# KNIGHTS AT TOURNAMENT

*Text by*
CHRISTOPHER GRAVETT
*Colour plates by*
ANGUS McBRIDE

First published in Great Britain in 1988 by
Osprey Publishing, Elms Court, Chapel Way, Botley,
Oxford OX2 9LP United Kingdom
Email: osprey@osprey-publishing.co.uk
Also published as Elite 17: *Knights at Tournament*.

ISBN 1 85532 937 9


Filmset in Great Britain
Printed in China through World Print Ltd.


FOR A CATALOGUE OF ALL BOOKS PUBLISHED BY OSPREY
MILITARY, AUTOMOTIVE AND AVIATION PLEASE WRITE TO:

The Marketing Manager, Osprey Direct USA, PO Box
130, Sterling Heights, MI 48311-0130, USA.
Email: info@OspreyDirectUSA.com

The Marketing Manager, Osprey Direct UK, PO Box
140, Wellingborough, Northants, NN8 4ZA, United
Kingdom.
Email: info@OspreyDirect.co.uk

Visit Osprey's website at:

http://www.osprey-publishing.co.uk

**Dedication:**
For my mother and father

**Acknowledgements:**
The author would like to thank the following for their
help in the preparation of this book: Dominique
Collon, Renate Gut, Ulrike Mundorff, Ann Payne,
Thom Richardson and Graeme Rimer.

COVER: 'Tournament at Smithfield, 1467' by
Graham Turner.

# Knights at Tournament

## Introduction

In this book I hope to trace the history of the tournament in its many forms, from its often brutal beginnings to the gaudy pageantry of the 15th and 16th centuries, and its final decline. The words 'tournament' and 'joust' are often used indiscriminately. Strictly speaking 'joust' describes single combat between two horsemen. 'Tournament' refers to the 'mêlée' or mounted combat between parties of knights, but could be used also to encompass the whole of the proceedings. Both types of martial exercise might be termed '*hastiludia*' ('spear play').

The word 'tournament' is itself obscure. Fauchet, writing in the 16th century, suggested it came from the fact that the knights ran at the quintain '*par tour*' or by turn. Others thought it came from the way parties of knights circled round before engaging. The late 12th century chronicler William Fitzstephen noted that knights were well trained to perform the necessary turnings and evolutions in martial sports.

The origins of the tournament are something of a mystery. No doubt it derived from the military games in which all warrior classes have engaged as a preparation for war. However, we do not know when or where this became focused in a particular activity. The tournament was essentially a mounted sport; it may derive ultimately from the Roman 'Troy Game' (*ludus Troiae*) or the military sports among the German tribes mentioned by Tacitus, Virgil and Suetonius, in which groups of warriors fought mock battles. Though cavalry was little used in much of central and western Europe after the fall of the Roman Empire, Frankish rulers began to place greater emphasis on horsemen during the 8th century. The medieval tournament does not appear to have come into being before the middle of the 10th century. In a chronicle from the abbey of St.

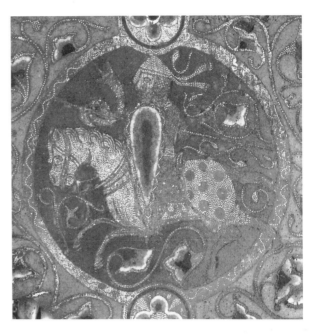

In early tournaments the participants fought in the same armour in which they went to war. This mailed knight appears on a Limoges casket of the second half of the 12th century. The '*infulae*' hanging from the back of the helmet may denote rank. (Reproduced by courtesy of the Trustees of the British Museum.)

Martin at Tours under the year 1066 comes a reference to one Godfrey de Preuilly, who is said to have been killed in a tournament for which he made the rules.

Tournaments appear to have evolved on the European mainland. Osbert of Arden, writing in the reign of Henry I, mentions the coloured lances he took over the sea to tourney. In his *Expugnatio Hibernica* Gerald of Wales notes knights making passes 'as if practising for tournaments of the French sort'. Moreover, the 13th century chronicler Matthew Paris refers to tournaments as '*Conflictus Gallicus*' and '*batailles francaises*'. Otto of Freising notes how, in 1146, the French mocked the Germans for their lack of horsemanship. He does, however, mention a tourney at Würzburg in 1127. William of Newburgh, writing in 1197, maintains

3

**A German knight from the Manessa Codex _c._1300. The coronel-headed lance carries a vamplate to guard the hand, and a 'graper' to wedge it under the arm and prevent it slipping backwards on impact. (Universitäts-Bibliothek, Heidelberg.)**

# The 12th and 13th Centuries

During the 12th century the tournament remained a highly dangerous mêlée. The 'lists' at this time referred not to the enclosure in which a tournament took place, but to fenced or roped refuges set up at either end of a vast concourse of open countryside, dotted about with further areas designated for recuperation. The word is obscure; it may derive from the '_lis_', the French royal court at which martial games were held. Alternatively it might come from '_licium_' (band of material) or '_palicium_' (paling) surrounding the lists. The battlefield was usually described as being between two towns, and sometimes villages were not excluded from the area. The reference to Godfrey de Preuilly suggests that there were now certain rules by which the knights participating had to abide. However, the great size of the field precluded efficient supervision by marshals or judges. Men were still often killed or wounded during the course of such spectacles. The weapons used were those of actual warfare; there is no mention of the use of special blunted versions.

The best reference to the tournament at this time is the biography of William Marshal, who became Marshal of England. The work was written in the second quarter of the 13th century by the old man's squire with the help of a _trouvère_. It graphically illustrates how a young man could use his skill at arms to seize ransoms and amass wealth by 'doing the circuit'.

About two weeks' notice was given by messenger, and the combatants were divided into two teams usually with reference to area or nationality. Normans and English often combined against the French. Those arriving alone either joined a contingent or formed a temporary company of their own. The knights slept little the night before the event, attending to their harness and equipment, and rolling the mail hauberks in barrels of sand to polish them.

'Commencements'—perhaps a form of procession—opened the proceedings. In the mêlée it was not considered unchivalrous for several knights to attack a single opponent, nor for mounted men to charge those who had been unhorsed and were now fighting on foot. Some lords

that tournaments first arrived in England during the reign of Stephen (1135–1154).

During the 12th century the popularity of tournaments increased enormously. They may have passed to Italy in mid-century from the German Empire; a large gathering even took place at Antioch in Syria, the Byzantine Emperor himself taking part.

Early allusions to '_tornoi_' often appear in accounts of real war, and it is interesting that the increase in references to tournaments coincides with the universal adoption of the mounted charge with the lance 'couched' under the arm. This suggests that tourneys were now forming a substantial part of knightly training for war. Richard I licensed them in England, so William of Newburgh tells us, because he noted the superiority of the French knights. Galbert of Bruges relates that Charles, Count of Flanders (died 1127) used tournaments to keep his knights in trim and to gain glory. In the 13th century Henri de Laon actually believed tournaments were becoming too soft, so losing their usefulness as exercises for war!

employed footsoldiers to fend off unwanted attacks. When William became the guardian of Henry II's son, the 'Young King', the pair attended a number of tourneys in France. We read of William confronting opponents on palisaded mounds and in farm buildings, village streets and vineyards.

Though great lords often appear to have fought for honour, others took part in order to seize booty. In his first tourney William overthrew one knight, taking his pledge for ransom before capturing three others. He shared a fifth prisoner with another knight, and came away with 'four and a half' horses, with as many riding mounts for squires, plus baggage horses and equipment. After unseating an opponent it was sometimes prudent to take only his horse. William was about to capture a knight whom he had unhorsed when five others attacked him. As he beat them off, his helmet came adrift and turned round, forcing him to withdraw to the lists, where he had the greatest difficulty in removing it. One prisoner, while being led back by William after capture in the town of Anet, grabbed an overhanging drainpipe and swung up out of his saddle: on turning round William discovered his prisoner had vanished—an incident which occasioned much laughter.

It was often advantageous to wait until the opposing team was battered and dazed by blows to the helmet. The leading men were then more vulnerable to capture, and a number of prisoners could be seized without disrupting the combat group. Once rendered *hors de combat*, prisoners could then be led (on their horses) to the squires. Their parole was expected but occasionally broken. Combat went on until dusk, when the knights gathered to discuss the event and to decide who had earned the prize. After one tourney two knights accompanied a squire bearing a brooch to present to William Marshal. He was found eventually with his head on an anvil, while hammers and pincers were used to extricate him from his battered helmet!

The ransom of companions needed attention,

**Knights jousting, from an ivory box lid of the first half of the 14th century. Trumpeters representing each combatant sound their instruments to encourage the knights. *The Siege of the Castle of Love*, an allegory illustrated here, gives some idea of the '*Scharmützel*', an assault on a wooden fortress especially constructed for the lists. In reality it is highly unlikely that ladies would defend even these sham strongholds. (Reproduced by courtesy of the Trustees of the British Museum.)**

and details for disposal of prisoners and equipment might be worked out beforehand. The final word appears to have rested with the team leader; ransoms tended to be lighter than those in war. In 1177 William joined a Flemish knight named Roger de Gaugi in a partnership during which 103 prisoners were taken in ten months. The great affair at Lagny in 1179 was William's last tourney: the Young King's household was increased to 200, including 11 knights banneret. The Duke of Burgundy and 13 counts also attended.

By the end of the 12th century retinues were diminishing in size, but there are still references to the use of darts, crossbow bolts and bodies of footsoldiers in the tourney. Fitzstephen describes young Londoners and noble youths not yet knighted indulging in mounted combat with shields and headless lances. This may be a type of 'Behourd', a less formal diminutive of the tourney which was not proclaimed beforehand (though it has been suggested that the word refers to an attack on a sham wooden castle). Fitzstephen also mentions combat on the frozen Thames. In 13th century Tuscany and Umbria soldiers of the communal levies took part in the '*Giuoco del Mazzascuto*', a foot combat with shields and clubs which outlasted the tournament.

In Germany the gatherings were taken over by the emperor or princes as symbols of pomp. English

**A judicial combat as depicted on a 13th century tile from Chertsey abbey. Unarmoured and carrying rectangular shields fitted with central bosses, the combatants use a type of pick. This style of combat was employed in civil and in certain criminal cases.**

kings were generally wary of allowing tournaments to be staged—the occasion might easily be used to cloak the beginnings of a revolt. Apparently an attack on Alençon was repulsed when those participating in a nearby tourney were enlisted to help, giving some idea of how many fighting men were assembled together. Henry II issued edicts against such sports, and William of Newburgh observes that many young knights travelled abroad to seek tourneys, especially in France. According to Jocelyn of Brakelond the sport was revived in England by Richard I, who licensed tourneys to be held in five places only; henceforward, to hold an unlicensed tournament was regarded as an offence against the crown. Always in need of money to finance his military enterprises, Richard allowed entry to such gatherings only on payment of a sum befitting rank. An earl was to pay 20 marks of silver; a baron ten marks; a landed knight four marks; a landless knight two. The Chief Justice appointed his brother to collect these payments, and two knights and two clerks attended each tourney to ensure that the king's wishes were carried out.

There were bouts of illegal tourneying after any baronial disturbance or quarrel with royal favourites. A tournament was planned after King John's capitulation at Runnymede. Some were between sides representing the court and the barons, and virtually lapsed into civil war. Henry III (1216–1272) decreed that all who held unlicensed tourneys were to lose their estates and their children were to be disinherited. When he knighted 80 aspirants they all went abroad to tourney, accompanied by the king's son, Prince Edward. After the Battle of Evesham tourneying again found royal favour, especially under the warlike Edward I, who had distinguished himself at a meeting at Blei in 1256. When events were banned there was usually a reason: the king was either absent abroad, or needed his barons for a war.

Philip II of France (1180–1223) forbade his sons to take part in tournaments because of the danger to life and limb (though the king was not noted for his courage). In any case, kings could turn tournaments to their own advantage by staging the most lavish spectacles themselves. In this way they could survey their baronage, promote their own splendour, and recruit fighting men in the same way as the aristocracy.

## The Church

The Church had consistently opposed tournaments, issuing prohibitions in 1131, 1139 and 1179. In 1193 Pope Celestine III's edict was followed almost immediately by Richard I's granting of licences. The ban on church burial for those killed in the tourney might be sidestepped by surviving long enough to put on monkish garb, as did Eustace de Calquille in 1193. In 1228 Pope Gregory IX promulgated another bull, but without success. The papacy disliked the way the tournament promoted activity in a turbulent baronage. The casualties incurred in these games continued to be a major obstacle to papal approval, though the Church began to emphasize other reasons. Three members of the Count of Holland's family were trampled to death within 15 years during the 1220s and 1230s. Dietrich, Margraf of Meissen died in 1176 and Geoffrey, son of Henry II of England, in 1186. William Marshal's son, Gilbert, was killed in 1241. In 1175 it is reported that 17 knights died in a German tournament, prompting the Archbishop of Magdeburg to campaign against the '*pestifer ludus torneamentorum*'. William Marshal's biography says that the French disliked fighting in cold weather; but in 1240 no less than 60 combatants died at a tournament held at Neuss near Cologne, many suffocated by heat and dust.

The practice of using teams from specific areas was liable to instil thoughts of revenge. English

An early 14th century illustration of a mêlée with swords. The Church could never really associate itself with the bloodshed frequently encountered in the tournament: here devils hover ready to snatch the souls of any knights killed during the proceedings. (By permission of the British Library.)

knights at the Rochester tournament of 1251 nursed a grudge against foreigners for the treatment some of them had received abroad. The event degenerated into a real battle; the visiting continentals were beaten with staves and chased into the town by the squires. Two years later the Earl of Gloucester's party was so well pounded at a foreign tournament that they needed medical attention and baths before they could attempt to return to England. Even the king might become embroiled in these undignified scrums. In 1274 Edward I, returning from the Holy Land, was invited by the Count of Châlons to take part in a tourney. As the combat warmed up the count grabbed Edward by the neck and tried to pull him off his horse. Furious, the king swung at his opponent and managed to drag him unceremoniously from his mount. Angered at this sight, the French knights turned the tournament into a real fight which was exacerbated by the participation of footsoldiers and spectators who were not supposed to interfere. When order was finally restored the count acknowledged Edward the victor of 'La petite Bataille de Châlons'. It soon became illegal to lay hands on an opponent.

The Church feared for the souls of combatants. At Neuss demons were heard crying as they flew

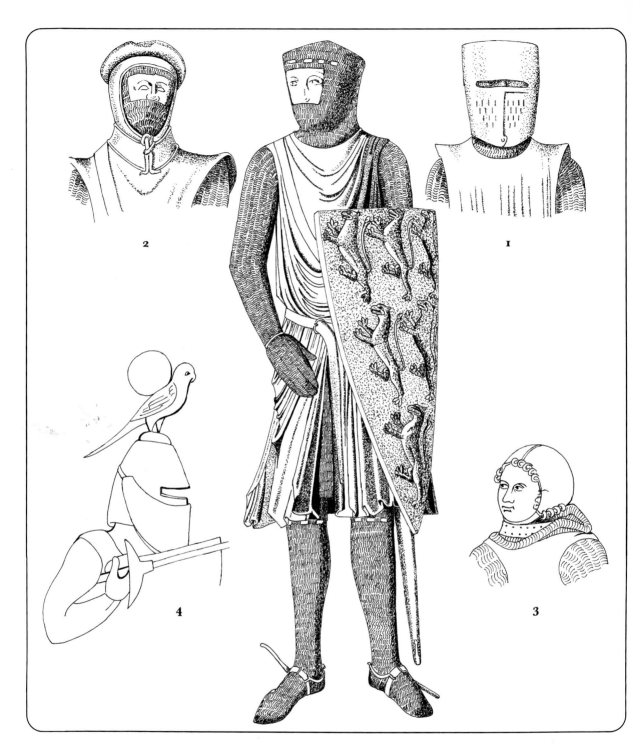

Armour worn in tournaments of the first half of the 13th century differed little from that used in war. Mail covers most of the body and a surcoat might carry a coat of arms. The figure is from the tomb of William, Earl of Salisbury and dates to about 1240. The contemporary figures on Wells cathedral show: (1) an early helm; (2) the arming cap with a padded roll to support the helm. The throat collar is here worn over the mail. (3) a figure from the Mackiejowski Bible (French *c.*1250) revealing a collar worn under the mail; (4) by about 1300 a plate 'barber' was sometimes strapped over the lower part of the helm as shown in the German *Manessa Codex*.

over the field in the guise of crows and vultures. Those who lost might exact reparation from their own subjects or, as Ulrich von Liechtenstein observed at Friesach, pawn their goods to Jews in order to raise ransom money. The Lord of Hemricourt constantly mortgaged his lands and plate to indulge in the increasingly costly sport.

Participation was now becoming too expensive for poorer knights, and lords were forced to entertain ever more lavishly.

Many did not see the harm in the tourney, however. At Chauvency (1285) and the contemporary meeting at Hem-sur-Somme, mass was attended before and after the event. A popular story told of a knight who, en route to a tournament, stopped to pray to the Virgin and thereby missed the combat. On arrival he was acclaimed, and realised that the Virgin herself had jousted in his place. The Church might try to emulate royal rulers in using tournaments to seize a person wanted for an offence which was difficult to prove. The patronage of the higher nobility always obstructed the enforcement of church bans. The bull of 1279 was revoked by Pope Martin IV in 1281, but not until the pontificate of Clement VI (1342–52) were tournaments allowed as part of the festivities at the papal court at Avignon. The Church had long feared that tournaments stirred up the warrior classes who should be fighting for Christian ethics preferably on crusade. In fact tournaments were sometimes useful in gathering warriors in order to promote a crusade, as happened at Écry in 1199 and Trazegnies in 1251.

## Civilising Attitudes

The 'Statuta de Armis' or 'Statutum Armorum in Torniamentis' reveals that at least by the later 13th century some substantial rules were in circulation in England. That this was not the case previously is suggested by the fact that these rules were ordered by the king at the request of the barons. Any knight or squire breaking these rules was liable to lose horse and armour and be imprisoned for three years. Any member of the nobility found wanting would be hauled before the 'seigneurs' at a court of honour with powers to seize horse, armour and liberty. In an attempt to control violent behaviour by spectators the Statute forbade them to attend in armour or carrying weapons. The unruly behaviour of squires was a prime consideration. Their 'behourds' were banned in 1234. At Boston Fair in 1288 two gangs of squires, dressed as monks, burnt down part of the town. The ordinance specified that no count, baron or knight was to have more than three armed squires who had to wear their master's badge (Ulrich von Liechtenstein mentions having

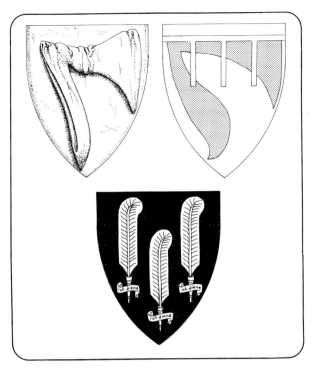

Some 13th century texts speak of a lady's sleeve being worn on the shield as a token; the heraldic 'maunch' was probably derived from this. At the Dunstable tournament in 1308 Sir Nicholas Hastings bore a red *maunch* on gold, with a blue label of three points. The shield of peace of Edward, the Black Prince (died 1376) was used for jousts of courtesy with blunt lances. The predominance of black on shield and surcoat gave him his nickname. His shield of war bore the royal arms.

four squires in uniform clothing). A squire might only assist the knight whose device he wore, and no knight or squire might use pointed sword or dagger, staff or baston, only broadswords for the tourney.

During the 13th century an alternative form of lance appeared. The 'lance of peace' was either rebated or else provided with a 'coronel'—an iron head ending in three points which spread the force of impact instead of concentrating it all in one place. This and the rebated sword were known as 'arms of courtesy' (*à plaisance*). The 'lance of war' (*à outrance*) was fitted with the usual sharp head, the contest ending when one combatant was killed or disabled. However, the fight could be stopped if so desired, and some contests were held solely to display skill and courage with such weapons.

The introduction of rebated arms indicates a move towards safety. Normal armour was often worn; at Chauvency shin and arm defences and iron throat collars are mentioned. At the same time there is evidence for the use of lighter armour, especially, it seems, at 'behourds'. The earliest mention of this armour occurs in a reference by Matthew Paris. A much more detailed account is found in the Roll of Purchases for the Windsor Park tourney in 1278. At this event the 38 combatants included the earls of Cornwall, Gloucester, Lincoln, Pembroke, Richmond and Warenne, as well as several foreign knights. Armour and weapons were provided for all, costing from seven to 25 shillings, only Lincoln receiving harness worth 33s 4d. Armour and even helms were of leather while whalebone swords were covered in parchment and silvered: swords cost 7d, but a charge of 25s was made for silvering all 38 blades, and 3s 6d for gilding the hilts. Carriage from

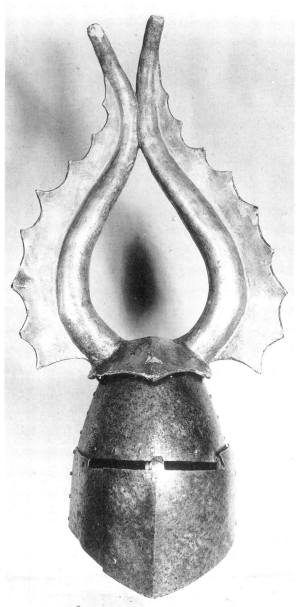

London for all the equipment came to 3s, and total cost was £80 11s 8d. There is no mention of lances. The appearance at tournaments of '*diseurs*' or judges suggests that the field was now more restricted in size.

Bourgeois tourneys such as the meeting at Magdeburg in 1281 were respected by the nobility. However, during the 13th century the first move to regulate tournaments was to remove undesirables from them; this led to further restrictions on those who could not prove knightly forebears.

Ulrich von Liechenstein, writing of the German tournament in the first half of the 13th century, noted with satisfaction how one meeting had been free from low-minded nobles; the true knight sought honour. Ransom was still eagerly pursued, especially in the smaller contests, and events were plentiful; Ulrich attended 12 in one summer. His description of the mass charge reveals knights grouped under the banners of their respective lords and then divided into two teams. The haphazard changes of fortune, however, certainly owe more to the battlefield than a dignified contest. In one mêlée Ulrich and his troop used their lances and broke through the squadron of Hadmar von Kühnringe. Surrounded, Hadmar's men still managed to capture three of their opponents before the latter could turn their horses. Seeing Hadmar's plight, his brother led a charge with levelled lances and rammed the horses of Ulrich's knights. Now the latter's group was surrounded, until he in turn was assisted by the band of Wolfger von Gors. In this contest there is no mention of swordplay. Ulrich informs us that he used nine lances, whilst Sir Wolfger and Sir Engelschalk broke many spears. As in the tourneys of William Marshal, the fighting went on until darkness fell. Ulrich then rode back to the inns and found the prisoners he had captured; presumably his squires had taken them from the field.

German romances, such as Wolfram von

**The Pranke helm, so called because it belonged to a member of the Pranke family from Styria. Dating from the mid-14th century, it bears a reinforcing plate on the wearer's left side below the vision slit, suggesting that the helm was used for jousting rather than warfare. The buffalo horn crest is not contemporary, but probably dates from the early 15th century. It is made of wood, as are several other such crests. However, another buffalo horn crest preserved in Cherbourg castle is made of *cuir bouilli*, the hollow horns being sewn on to the leather cap, and the whole covered in canvas and gesso before being painted at a later date. (Waffensammlung, Vienna.)**

Eschenbach's *Parzival*, provide further information. In German lands it would appear there were five different courses from which the competitor might choose. '*Diu volge*' is rather obscure. '*Zen muoten*' appears to have involved a single knight attacking a group, trying to unhorse one opponent whilst avoiding the others. '*Zem puneiz*' refers to the charge in the mêlée, whilst '*zem treviers*' necessitated the team turning 45 degrees to the right to take the opposing knights on the open side, avoiding the lance. The manoeuvre could only be done at the last possible moment in order to achieve surprise. '*Ze rehter tjost*' was the joust between two knights.

## The Joust

The word 'joust' or 'just' probably derives from the Latin '*juxtare*'—to meet together. It had one great advantage over the tournament: a knight might show off his skill in single combat without becoming entangled with several other participants. Jousting had sometimes occurred before the mêlée proper in the time of William Marshal and it is mentioned by William of Malmesbury in the 12th century; but it was not until the second half of the 13th century that it came to the fore. Its popularity was probably assisted by literary references to judicial duels between good and evil. Again, the German romances provide some idea of procedure. The point of aim was either the four nails on the shield, or the helm or throat armour. Ulrich von Liechtenstein tells of a number of jousts where riders were hit on the throat collar (Ulrich's was of iron). We hear of collars being split or having large holes punched in them: in one joust Ulrich pierced his opponent's collar through shield and mail, sending the knight flying from the saddle to land bleeding and half-dead some distance from his horse. We are also told how Ulrich's squires each carried three lances bound with a thong. They were often coloured; one rider had a band of tiny bells fastened to his lance, complementing those festooning his body.

Usually three lances could be broken, but fighting on horseback with swords was virtually unknown. Removing the helm signified a wish to end the joust. If the contestants desired to proceed beyond the three lances, both could dismount and a swordfight was begun on foot. If one was unhorsed by a lance thrust but not seriously hurt, the other would dismount to continue. Some knights were so eager to attack Ulrich that they advanced three at a time, which the author considered bad manners. We hear of shields shattered by the lance or sent flying when the thongs burst; in one encounter a lance penetrated shield and mail and wounded Ulrich in the chest. Not all contestants were skilled; one knight missed ten times and ended up hitting Ulrich's horse in the head, badly wounding the animal. On another occasion a knight dropped his lancehead too low and struck Ulrich's horse in the neck, causing the animal to rear and throw its rider. In this period horses were set at a gallop in order to achieve maximum momentum for the clash; Ulrich not only speaks of lengthy runs taken to achieve effect, he notes how one knight failed to break his lance because he rode too slowly. When both galloped hard the desired effect was achieved.

Later 13th century tournaments show a definite order, illustrated by the description of events at Chauvency in September 1285. It appears that invitations were sent at least three weeks before the event. The author, Jacques de Britex, records that a grand fête on the Sunday was followed by two days of jousting. Though the number participating is unknown, the account of the tourney at Hem shows that here 180 runs were made in two days. At

An encampment before a tournament, *c.*1360. Large gatherings must have sprouted numerous tents and pavilions, since only the highest lords would be able to lodge in the nearby town or castle. At a meeting in Westminster in 1501 tents for participants were erected in the lists and removed before jousting began. (By permission of the British Library.)

Chauvency heralds and kings-of-arms identified coats-of-arms and cried the names and in some instances the war-cries of individual combatants. They also answered questions put by ladies in the stands. On the Wednesday a mêlée was proclaimed for the following afternoon, so that darkness would force the action to cease. No mêlée is mentioned at Hem.

## Ladies

Evidence for the presence of ladies at 12th century tournaments is slight. In Geoffrey of Monmouth's *History of the Kings of Britain* of c. 1140 we hear of ladies on the battlements urging on the knights engaged below. Whilst waiting for one tourney to begin, William Marshal sang while the knights and ladies of the retinue of the Countess of Loigni danced. A minstrel composed a song in which he asked for a horse; William mounted, overthrew the first knight who opposed him, and presented the animal to the minstrel. In the early 13th century

**Philippe de Ternant, depicted in armour for the mêlée, from the 'Armorial equestre' of about 1450. The order of the Golden Fleece hangs round his neck. Both the saddle bow and the chanfron on the horse's head repeat his arms: checky or and gules (gold and red).**

*Lancelot* by Chrétien de Troyes, ladies become patronesses of the tourney; patrons of literature might also support tournaments, bringing the spectacle of romance to the violent world of warriors.

The rise of the ideals of courtly love, which first appeared in southern France during the 12th century, and the romances (especially of King Arthur's knights) which blossomed in the 13th, brought to the fore notions of courtesy and chivalry. It is hardly surprising, then, that jousting began to rise in popularity in the 13th century. There was an increasing awareness that honour should be done to a lady by her champion—as portrayed in the romantic literature. Perhaps the most extreme example of this trend is the picture of Ulrich von Liechtenstein, who related his jousting tour of the Holy Roman Empire dressed as a lady, complete with false tresses. Much debate has centred on just how this outrageous journey was received at the various stopping places, and how much fiction is woven into the facts.

He mentions that knights took part in the mass mêlée in order to honour the ladies, suggesting that jousting was not the sole method of winning admiration and that the mêlée was becoming more restricted in size. We may also note how some tourney fields were rather makeshift. In one incident Ulrich watched from a hostelry balcony, and since he was dressed as a woman this presumes that special stands were not an automatic requisite at this time. Nonetheless, women were now featuring more and more in the panoply of the tourney. As a condition of jousting during his tour, Ulrich demanded that any knight whom he unhorsed should bow to the four corners of the world in honour of a lady. Those breaking a spear against him received a gold ring to give to their lady. Jacques de Vitry speaks of 'tokens' from ladies dresses being carried as 'favours'; a veil might be worn round the helm or on the lance. The final joust began to be dedicated to the ladies. Ulrich notes how at the marriage of the daughter of Prince Leopold of Austria, the tourney was followed by dances and many other knightly games.

Courtly and amorous appeal could also be extended into areas of ceremony, theatre and play. At Chauvency the interludes between festivities included the 'robardel' game in which two girls dressed as shepherd and shepherdess mimed the story of the theft of a kiss. Fantasy was establishing itself; one of Ulrich's opponents came to the field in a monk's black robes, bearing a tonsured wig on his helmet! Ulrich's other work, the *Artusfahrt*, tells of his adventures disguised as King Arthur with six others in appropriate dress. Anyone breaking a lance was admitted to the 'Round Table'. Arthur was a popular figure to be used in the emerging ceremonial; the earliest reference is in a tournament in Cyprus in 1223. Sarasin relates how, at Hem, the sister of one of the organisers, Aubert de Longueval, was dressed as Guinevere while Robert Count of Artois, as Yvain, rescued four damsels from the 'Knight of the White Tower'. When Edward I held a similar tourney in 1299 a squire dressed up as the 'loathly damsel'.

## The Round Table

Mock warfare had been known in England from at least 1216 but, as the name implies, the 'Round Table' offered more. In the mid-12th century it was already alluded to by Wace, suggesting that by that date it was familiar to his audience. The tradition of King Arthur was by this time known to the knightly circles in England, and here the Arthurian cult most easily transferred itself to the lists. This cult had been known to those moving in the court circle of Richard I. It had also crossed the Channel. In 1235 a Round Table was held at Hesdin in Flanders, whilst in 1281 at Magdeburg merchants and townsmen met at Pentecost. By the end of the 13th century the similar '*Gral*' tournaments had appeared, to which knights were invited to try their skills. They were connected with spring festivals and took place in May or Whitsuntide (Ulrich went to Friesach in 1224 as 'King May'). Such events never generally took hold in the Empire, however. In 1286 a Round Table was held at Acre in the Holy Land; at '*La raine de Femenie*' the jousters dressed as women, monks, nuns or Arthurian characters.

The first mention in public records of the game known as the 'Round Table' is under the year 1232. On that occasion the meeting, at an unspecified location, was banned because of a Welsh expedition. There is no distinction here between the Round Table and any other form of tournament. However, Matthew Paris, writing of the games at Wallenden in 1252, calls this form the '*Mensa Rotunda*' and distinguishes it from the tournament

Fighting at the barriers during a siege, from an illumination of *c.*1400. Although foot combat across a wooden bar was not introduced until the end of the 15th century, it was considered necessary during a siege if both sides agreed to entertain themselves with trials of strength. The barrier would discourage surprise attack by the besiegers and sorties by the besieged, as well as any thoughts of seizing hostages from among the participants. Here the knights wear their normal war gear, including bascinet with 'hounskull' visor. The crested great helm was now becoming relegated to the lists. (**By permission of the British Library.**)

('*torneamentum quasi hostile*'). Unfortunately he does not elaborate on this distinction. It would seem likely that at the Round Table only rebated weapons were used. Matthew recounts how on the fourth day a knight called Arnold de Montigny was killed when his throat was pierced by the lance of Roger de Leyburne 'which had not been blunted as it ought to have been'; the lance-head remained in the wound and soon proved fatal. Since Roger had suffered a broken leg in an earlier tournament when riding against Arnold, his motives here were somewhat suspect. The *Prose Tristan* of about 1232 says that the banner of the Round Table is not that of mortal battle, whilst a source of 1235 notes it was a strictly regulated joust. It seems likely that there was no mêlée in which tempers might fray too easily. The use of blunted weapons fitted the occasion, since the Round Table was not just a contest of martial skill, but rather a social gathering of ladies and gentlemen in which jousting formed only a part of the proceedings. The Warwick Round Table 'sat' in 1257, suggesting that the combat was not the only item on the agenda. The famous Round Table of 1279 at Kenilworth was held under the auspices of Roger Mortimer. Over three days and at great expense he invited 100 knights and many ladies. The prize, a golden lion, was awarded to the host himself!

In 1284 Edward I organised a Round Table in Caernarvonshire to celebrate his conquest of Wales. These meetings continued into the 14th century, culminating in the great festivities held at Windsor by Edward III in 1344. Two kings and two queens, the Prince of Wales, a duke, ten earls, nine countesses and numerous others came from places as far apart as Scotland and Germany, and the event lasted for 15 days. In 1348 or 1349 Edward held a Round Table at Lichfield. The challengers or 'tenans' included the king and 17 knights; the

**The king-of-arms of the Duke of Brittany before the Duke of Bourbon, from the tract on tournaments by René of Anjou. The duke holds a blunt tourney sword which he has taken from the king-of-arms in acceptance of the challenge. Now he studies a roll on which are emblazoned the shields of several men of sound calibre, from which it is hoped he will pick two knights and two squires to act as judges in the forthcoming proceedings. The illustrations were probably executed in about 1460. (Bibliothèque Nationale, Paris.)**

visitors or '*venans*' were the Earl of Lancaster and 14 knights. At this affair the king jousted wearing the arms of Sir Thomas Bradeston. Although the Round Table continued to figure as a social gathering it declined in frequency after the mid-14th century.

## The Quintain and Ring

The quintain was a target against which warriors could practise. It was known at least as far back as Roman times, and might be a simple wooden post. For mounted lancers, a form developed consisting of a post with a revolving arm on top. To one end of the arm was affixed a shield, to the other a heavy weight such as a sand bag. Once the shield was struck, the weight swung round; anyone not fast enough in riding by received a solid blow on the back. One type substituted a swinging figure (often a Saracen) sometimes holding a wooden sword. If struck cleanly between the eyes the quintain was apparently prevented from turning properly. Non-knightly classes might have a quintain set up on the village green. Other versions included a shield fixed to a pole placed in a river, the jouster standing in the prow of a rowing boat (first mentioned by Fitzstephen in the late 12th century). This diversion extended to actual jousts between boats—Elizabeth I witnessed one such event at Sandwich in 1573.

Running at the ring ('*Ringelrennen*' or the '*Corso all' Annello*') entailed galloping towards a ring hanging from an upright with the object of carrying it off on the lance. The latter was shorter than that used in jousting; one 17th century example is 10ft 7 in. long and weighs 7lb. It is tipped with a cone to hold the ring, but for obvious reasons it has no vamplate to guard the hand. Sometimes the fluted shafts of these later lances were decorated with pierced work. This sport became popular especially in the 16th and 17th centuries, notably at the court of Louis XIV.

The lodgings of the combatants during a tournament, from René of Anjou's book. The large pennon advertises the leader. Tourneyers must give four days notice to the heralds, who organised the painting of the wooden boards with the arms of the two teams. For each board and banner they were paid four *sous parisiennes*. Traditionally heralds received '*clouage*' (nail money) for nailing up the arms of participants at tournaments. They might also be entitled to the armour of those entering the lists with no right, as well as armour or horses which fell to the earth during combat and which the owners could later redeem with a fee. Additionally, those participating in the lists for the first time were expected to donate their helmet to the heralds. Those taking part in their first joust were exempted if they had been in the tourney (i.e. the mêlée). The reverse was not the case, however, indicating that the tourney was still regarded as a superior contest. In the 16th century this custom was usually commuted to a money payment, or scarves or plumes in the nobleman's colours. '**Largesse**' was always cried by heralds. (**Bibliothèque Nationale, Paris.**)

# The 14th Century

Unlike Henry III in the 13th century, the warlike Edward III was prepared to accept tournaments. The fact that they were now becoming better regulated no doubt assisted this decision. Shortly after the Windsor Round Table of 1344 he issued letters patent for '*hastiludia*' and jousts to be allowed annually at Lincoln, both in time of war and of peace. The Earl of Derby was nominated 'Captain' ('*Capitaneus*') of a tournament for life, the post to be elective thereafter.

The 'tonlet' as described and illustrated in René of Anjou's treatise in the mid-15th century consisted of a cuirass and fauld, the former pierced for lightness and ventilation. It was large enough for a pourpoint to be worn beneath, three fingers thick at the shoulder, arms and back. The tonlet was worn under the tabard during the club tourney. The helmet takes to pieces; the leather crest base is fitted with an iron spike to take the crest. René notes that the helm could be attached to the chest by a chain. In Flanders, Hainault and Germany the helm was worn over an open bascinet and camail which was tied down. There the demi-pourpoint was covered by a bodice stuffed four fingers deep with cotton on which were fixed the arm pieces, of *cuir bouilli* stiffened by sticks glued to them. Shoulder and elbow pieces were heavy and stuffed inside with a double stitched thickness. Over all this came a light brigandine and tabard, making René remark that such tourneyers appeared wider than they were tall, and could hardly turn their horses! De la Sale records that varlets would strike their masters' arms and shoulders with clubs to test the effectiveness of the armour.

Royal jousts often celebrated princely weddings or coronations and were proclaimed throughout Europe. Knights wishing to attend were provided with safe conducts as they journeyed across foreign territories. During the Hundred Years' War the Duke of Burgundy condemned a duel between the Seigneur de Clery and an English knight since permission had not been obtained to fight with the enemy. In his opinion it was an offence worthy of death, but the King of France eventually granted a pardon.

At such gatherings potential trouble could never be ruled out. In 1362 the town council in Nuremberg tried unsuccessfully to forbid the tournament because of the disturbances caused by the townspeople at these meetings. Yet increasingly the proceedings were becoming hedged around with formalities. One of the most famous tournaments of the time was that of St. Inglevert in 1389. It was proclaimed to be held near Calais on 20 May. Reynolde de Roy, Sir Boucicaut and the lord of St. Pye would have their lodgings there on the previous day, with their coats-of-arms displayed outside on shields of peace and of war. Anyone wishing to fight should either come himself or send a representative with a baton to touch the appropriate shield.

Officials would take the names, and the shields would not be covered with iron or steel.

The fighting itself was now becoming better regulated. Combat in the lists or *champ-clos* often consisted of three runs at the joust, and a similar number of blows with sword, axe or dagger. The number had a tendency to increase as the century wore on. At Montereau sur Yonne in 1387 five strokes each with the above weapons were allowed. The King of France was present, and saw Sir Thomas Harpenden knocked senseless after being unhorsed by Jean des Barres. However, he slowly recovered enough to enable the rest of the prescribed blows to be exchanged without further injury.

The chronicler Froissart, who recounts the above story, also furnishes an account of the proceedings at Entença where the Duke and Duchess of Lancaster presided, together with the King and Queen of Portugal. Sir John Holland had been challenged by

The inspection of the crested helmets of the combatants. Notice that the helmets are fitted with grilles for the tourney with clubs and blunt swords, and bear their owners' arms on the front. If any entrant was found to have dishonoured his name his helmet was removed, as seen on the right. The presiding herald is a freelance, distinguished by the numerous small shields on his tabard. (Bayerische Staatsbibliothek, Munich.)

a French knight to three runs in the joust and the same with axe, sword and dagger, for love of his lady. A herald bore the acceptance. The lists, a large close in the town, were well sanded and provided with galleries for the nobles. Sharp weapons had been agreed, and the two combatants stood a bow-shot apart. At the signal both charged and struck each other's visors; but whilst the Frenchman splintered his lance, his adversary struck off the helm, since it was only held by a single lace. When this happened again, and Sir John therefore had not broken a single lance, the English complained. They were told that Sir John had been

free to leave his own helm unsecured if he had so wished; it seems likely that loose fastenings were customary in Portugal and Spain. The rest of the contest went off without incident or hurt, and the Frenchman was adjudged the winner.

An unusual contest took place in 1398, when Lord Wells jousted with the Earl of Crawford on London Bridge. After the shock of the first course, the Earl remained so solidly in his saddle that people began to say he must be locked into it. To refute this charge, the Earl leapt down and remounted again with agility. On the third run Lord Wells was badly hurt when he was unhorsed. Injuries were still common enough; in 1390 John de Hastings, Earl of Pembroke, was mortally wounded in a practice joust when struck in the groin.

Pageantry increased throughout the century. Soon after the accession of Edward II (1307), Giles Argentine held the lists at Stepney as 'King of the Greenwood'. In 1343 challengers arrived at Smithfield dressed as the Pope and his cardinals. A crusading theme was conjured at a tournament in Paris (1385) by nominating one side as the knights of Richard Coeur de Lion and the other as Saladin and the Saracens. Bertrand du Guesclin attended a tourney with his face hidden by his helmet and with no heraldic markings on his shield: the idea of the 'unknown knight', popular in literature, was occasionally encountered in the lists—even Henry VIII appeared in this guise.

In 1331 Edward III joined a procession in which every knight was masked as a tartar and led by a lady with a gold chain. This idea is again encountered in 1339 when Jehan Bernier went to joust at the 'Espinette' at Lille accompanied by his own wife and those of three other men. Two led him into the lists by golden cords, whilst the other two each carried a lance. Similarly in 1390, during a procession to the Smithfield tournament, 60 ladies each led an armoured knight by a silver chain. Prizes after two days of jousting included a gold crown for the best lance among the *venans* and a gold clasp for that among the *tenans*. On the following day, a Tuesday, the lists were reserved for the squires. Prizes here included a fully accoutred charger for the best among the *venans*, and a falcon for the best of the *tenans*. The jousting was followed by a banquet and dancing till dawn. Wednesday saw jousting indiscriminately for knights and squires, while Thursday and Friday were reserved for fêtes, masques and banquets.

It was now expected that ladies would attend as a normal part of the proceedings. In the *Romance of Perceforest* we are told that they tore off pieces of clothing in their urge to furnish favours to the knights. 'Kerchiefs of plaisance' were worn by contestants as they had been earlier. A kiss might be claimed by the winner, or perhaps a 'gift of loving thanks'. The virginal belt (*'le gage d'amour sans fin'*), which a lady gave as token of her engagement to marry the knight, was later replaced by a garter bearing in French the words 'love without end'. Where one knight fought on behalf of one lady, the latter became 'the Queen of the Tournament'. In England during mid-century a band of about 50 ladies on fine horses and dressed in male clothing was noted as following every tourney, to the disgust of the Church. By the end of the century ladies were asked occasionally to choose the victor.

The tournament was slowly moving away from its parallels with real war. Nevertheless, in 1386 it was described by Ralf Ferrers as the place to find the school of arms. The mêlée still allowed for fighting on horseback with sword and mace; the lords of La Gruthuyse and Ghistelle led their allies in five 'lignes' or groups in the market place at Bruges in 1393. Yet the excessive costs now precluded young men from winning fame and fortune, and the onus on participants to prove their knightly background was becoming heavier. More and more the show became encased in formalities and ritual.

Manuscript illustrations and ivory carvings show that armour at first differed little from that used in battle. Extra pieces of plate armour were becoming more widespread for both war and tourney, but coronel-headed lances are frequently seen in illustrations of jousting knights. The de Nesle inventory of 1302 specifies whalebone shoulder pieces and hauberks for the tourney, while that of Roger de Mortimer (1322) suggests that helms were being made both for the joust and for tourney—unfortunately any differences are now lost to us. Early 14th century helms with added barbers seem to be shown in use by jousting knights; similarly, solid breastplates also occur in connection with jousting, as in an English royal wardrobe account of 1337–41. A heavy gauntlet or '*manifer*' to protect the

To the victor the spoils. The prize for the best combatant, in this case a jewel, is carried in a 'kerchief of plaisance' which itself is embroidered, garnished and spangled with gold. The kerchief has been used by the knight of honour to grant protection to participants during the mêlée. Preceded by trumpeters, it is now borne into the room by a chosen lady. The lady is flanked by two knightly judges, then by two young girls with the esquire judges. The king-of-arms makes a speech before he joins the heralds and pursuivants in shouting the winner's warcry. (Bibliothèque Nationale, Paris.)

left hand is also first mentioned in this account. The shield was sometimes laced to the shoulder, and instead of leg armour some jousters relied on a saddle with high recurving plates at the front. The lance was now being fitted with a large circular metal vamplate to guard the right hand.

## Jousting and Warfare

Occasionally both sides would engage in friendly contest in time of war, to win honour and boost the morale of their companions. Thus before the battle of Poitiers in 1356, a knight from Hainault called Eustace d'Aubrecicourt spurred out of the English ranks. His challenge was answered by a knight from Nassau, Louis de Recombes. They met at full speed and both fell, but the German was wounded in the shoulder. As Sir Eustace ran over to attack he was

Here shewes howe atte Coronacion of Quene Jane Erle Richard
kepte iuste for the Quenes part ayeynst all other comers wher
he so notably and so knyghtly behaved hym self, as redounded
to his noble fame and perpetuell worshyp

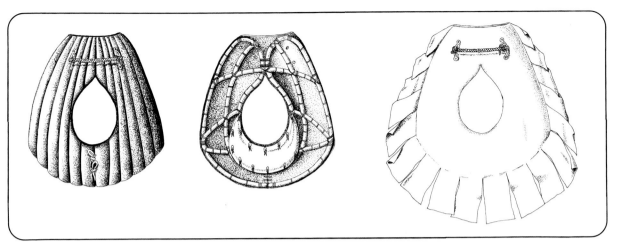

The '*hourt*' or defence for the horse's chest, as illustrated in the treatise of René of Anjou. Made with long straw stitched between strong canvas, the straw sack or 'bumper' is attached inside. On some illustrations the hourt is depicted without the horse trapper covering.

jumped by five German men-at-arms, hauled away and tied on a baggage-waggon. At the turn of the 16th century 13 Spanish and a similar number of French warriors fought during a truce between the armies at Monervyne in Italy. Anyone unhorsed would become a prisoner. The Spaniards aimed at the horses, but were still defeated.

Formal combat during sieges broke the monotony but could lead to trouble. At Bellême in 1113 knights rode out of the castle to test their skills. Some members of the besieging army had not heard of the truce ordered by Henry I, and attacked in force. The garrison knights fled back but the gate was jammed with men, and the town was taken. In 1420 mounted combats with lances even took place underground in the extensive mines laid by the English below Montereau. In one contest by the light of flambeaux and torches, the Sire de Brabanzon jousted with King Henry V until he realised his identity, after which he graciously retired. The occasion was conducted with great courtesy on both sides.

## The Judicial Duel

Combat to determine a man's guilt was found among the laws of many Germanic tribes, and persisted in medieval Europe. God, it was reasoned,

Richard Beauchamp, Earl of Warwick, performs a 'Joust of Peace'—from the *Beauchamp Pageants*. Though the tourney took place in 1403 the illustration dates to about 1480. The rider to the right of Sir Richard wears his master's livery with the badge of the ragged staff, repeated with its famous bear on the earl's crest. On the left the judges examine two lances to satisfy themselves that both weapons are identical. In another drawing Warwick's herald holds two saddles. Notice the 'graper' or spiked ring behind the handle of the broken lance, designed to dig into the wooden insert of the lance rest. (By permission of the British Library.)

would defend the innocent party. Even kings invoked it during disputes; thus Edward III challenged the King of France to combat between either two champions or 100 knights a side *à outrance*. In civil law cases (appeals over land) the defendant or *tenant* could, if he agreed to a combat, nominate a champion. The claimant ('*demandant*') had to use a champion, but if he won and it was found that the latter had been hired for a reward the suit was lost. The duel was fought on foot with no armour but a rectangular shield, together with a club tipped with horn or fitted with a double pickaxe head. The contest took place in a circular or oblong enclosure.

In England criminal cases involving murder could also be resolved in this way. At Valenciennes in 1455 a judicial combat took place following a murder accusation against a tailor. The arena was circular and provided with one entrance. Both men were placed in seats draped with black cloth, facing one another, and were sworn in. Their heads were shaven, feet bare, toe- and fingernails cut. Bodies, legs and arms were encased in boiled leather tightly laced down the middle. They had requested grease to wipe over the leather to hamper grappling, ashes to remove grease from the hands and assist the grip on their weapons, and a portion of sugar to hold in the mouth and absorb saliva. They each bore a pointed maplewood club and a shield. The tailor scooped up some of the sand with which the arena was strewn and flung it in his opponent's eyes before striking him in the face. The other in turn threw the

**Arming a man for combat on foot. This miniature of *c.*1480 from the Hastings manuscript shows the arming doublet worn under plate armour. It consists of a padded jacket with reinforcing gussets of mail to guard the armpit and elbow joint; a pair of mail pants protect the crotch. Padding would be wrapped round his knees beneath the metal, and shoes of thick cordwain would be worn. He is armed from the feet upwards. Behind may be seen other pieces of his equipment, including a bascinet fitted with the globose visor favoured in this type of contest. A pike and poleaxe rest against the wall. (Pierpont Morgan Library, M.775, f.122v.)**

tailor, put a knee on his stomach, and jabbed him between the eyes with his club until dead.

In Germany we may glimpse variations on the above themes. A bier, coffin, shroud and four candles were placed in the pavilion of each contestant. Illustrations by Paulus Kall include duellists who wear hooded one-piece white costumes bearing a black cross. Their shields, also with a cross, are long and rectangular and furnished with a varying number of spikes at top, bottom and sometimes sides. Daggers might be used in this form. Another combat utilised spiked clubs or swords, plus '*de Hutt*'—a shield shaped like a hat. Two-handed swords were also chosen for combat. In a form necessitating full armour, swords, daggers and spike-headed hammer were used. The *Gotha Codex* shows duellists previously anointed with oil by the armourer.

Criminal cases often involved matters of honour or allegations of treason, and the outcome was usually decided by mounted combat with sharp lances and swords. The appellant threw down a glove which the defendant picked up in token of acceptance. If the accusor failed to appear he was

outlawed. In the 'Gage of Battle' there was no set number of strokes, unlike the common practice in a tournament. Choice of weapons lay with the defendant, and they were inspected first. The contest began at sunrise; if no result was forthcoming by sunset the appellant lost. A 'perfect victory' required a confession of guilt.

In 1398 the famous confrontation between Henry Bolingbroke and Thomas Mowbray occurred, which Richard II stopped before the fight could begin. According to regulations promulgated by the Duke of Gloucester during this reign, the arena must be 60 paces long by 40 broad, the ground flat and hard, without large stones. It should be strongly barred with exits at east and west, the bars seven feet high to prevent a horse leaping them. Lance, long and short swords and daggers are permitted. Casting spears are mentioned sometimes, as in duels at Quesnoy in 1405 and Arras in 1431.

The judicial duel continued into the 16th century—the last so authorised in France took place in 1547—and was claimed in England as late as 1817. The law was repealed the following year.

# The 15th Century

During this century the tournament perhaps reached its zenith as a colourful spectacle spiced with danger. Holinshed relates that the threat of regicide had not completely disappeared. In 1400 the Earl of Huntingdon arranged a joust with his followers and those of the Earl of Salisbury, but a plot against Henry IV was uncovered. However, kings and princes no longer felt threatened by the tournament. On the contrary, they vied with each other to put on memorable displays, which contained more and more elements of fantasy. During the 15th century it was at the courts of Aix and Burgundy that the tournament perhaps found most favour; here it was transformed almost to a science. In Burgundy the sovereign used these occasions to keep in touch with his knights and army leaders, and to provide entertainment for his subjects, who often had to pay towards his wars and pageants.

The lavish extravagances of the Burgundian

court did not signify by any means that smaller gatherings were eclipsed. It should also be noted that bourgeois tournaments were popular, especially within Burgundian territory, hence the jousting societies in such places as Bruges, Tournai, and notably Lille, with its feast of the '*Espinette*'. Even Duke Philip the Good was prepared to joust with the bourgeois champions.

Italian tournaments were staged in every court which wanted to flaunt its wealth and social breeding, and formed useful vehicles for families like the Medici. In many cities such as Florence, Milan, Venice and even Rome, lavish spectacles were held in similar vein to those of the Burgundian court. In some versions towards the end of the 15th century the action was preceded by dramatic verse, as at Pesaro in 1475. Triumphal cars or 'pageants' were common; in 1466 the spectacle at Padua included a huge mounted figure of Jupiter, while in 1501 a ship was wheeled into one of the squares in Rome and assaulted.

In Germany the first half of the 15th century saw a remarkable lack of tourneying activity. Not until a meeting at Würzburg in 1479 did tournaments again become popular. Activities were largely in the hands of tournament societies such as those of Steinbock, Rüden and Esel, which closely monitored the ceremonious gatherings. Latterly the '*grossen Turniergesellschaft*' was formed from Swabia, Bavaria, Franconia and the Rhineland. The societies needed the backing of powerful nobles such as Graf Eberhard of Württemberg, who took part in a tourney at Stuttgart in 1484. The German nobility was not as wealthy as its Burgundian counterpart and so the spectacle was less fantastic. However, German princes took a keen interest in tournaments, often feeling it of great importance to be foremost in the contests. They kept horses especially for the occasion and made sure they were in fine fettle. Letters reveal that such animals were often requested for loan.

There was still a danger that in time of war tempers would boil over. In 1402 a contest *à outrance* was held at Orleans between knights of the Duke of Orleans and some English opponents. The duke ignored calls to stop it because of ill-feeling. The French chronicle charges the English with conceiving the strategy of allowing two of their number to overpower one Frenchman, but the plan misfired. An Englishman died, and a bitter and bloody fight

**Richard Beauchamp wounds Sir Pandolf Malatesta. Squires hover nearby with their masters' swords, holding them by the point to show they do not intend to join the fighting. The shattered remains of lances litter the sand. (By permission of the British Library.)**

**Since blunted tourney swords were used in the mêlée, armour in England consisted principally of a brigandine of small plates riveted inside a cloth cover. From the *Beauchamp Pageants*. (By permission of the British Library.)**

Armour of the late 15th century for combat on foot. A Milanese harness belonging to the Grand Chamberlain of Burgundy, it demonstrates the long, hooped skirt or 'tonlet' which remained popular for this type of contest until the mid-16th century. The 'bellows' visor is perforated with numerous holes and slits deliberately made small to obstruct entry by a weapon. The pauldrons on the shoulders are also especially wide. (Waffensammlung, Vienna.)

Even in time of peace the sport remained hazardous. When the Dukes of Burgundy and Brabant wished to joust at a tournament at Brussels in 1428 they were dissuaded by the kings-of-arms, who feared an accident. Two years later two knights were badly wounded in separate incidents in the market place at Arras when their visors were pierced.

Tournaments were still held to celebrate great occasions. At the coronation of Henry IV's queen in 1403 Richard Beauchamp, Earl of Warwick, jousted for the queen. He challenged Sir Pandolf Malatesta to joust followed by foot combat with axes, then with arming swords, and lastly with sharp daggers. Sir Pandolf was wounded in the shoulder and saved from death when the fight was stopped. In 1467 a tournament was held to celebrate the coronation of Edward IV, in which Lord Scales won the ring and ruby. For the entry of Louis XII into Paris a lily, 30 feet high and bedecked with the shields of the challengers, was erected in Paris.

Formalities extended to the challenge beforehand. Some knights wore an '*emprise*' or token which must be touched to signify a challenge accepted. Thus in 1400 a squire from Aragon fixed on a piece of leg armour and refused to remove it until someone accepted his challenge. In 1445 the Castilian Galiot de Baltasin arrived to challenge Philippe de Ternant. With the assent of the Duke of Burgundy, de Ternant attached a lady's lawn sleeve to his shoulder with a jewelled knot. Galiot asked the custom of the country, saying that where he came from the act of tearing the token off roughly denoted a fight to the death, but touching it signified a wish to fight for honour. De Ternant that same day sent sealed '*chapitres*' indicating the contests he desired.

## The Treatise of King René of Anjou

Of special interest for the history of the tournament is the *Traité de la forme et devis d'un tournoi* of René, King of Anjou. In penning the events of a fictional meeting at Aix in about 1440 he left minute details of the formalities surrounding the tournament as it existed in France, Germany, Flanders and Brabant, though the customs of the varying areas are included together.

The lord who decides to give the tournament

took place which the French finally won. Relations between English and French warriors became so bad that in 1409 the French king issued an ordinance forbidding all combats with sharp weapons. During a fight with axes in 1403 at Valencia a Spaniard grabbed a Frenchman by the leg and tried to knife him; the King of Aragon hastily threw down his baton to stop the fight.

calls his king-of-arms (or in his absence a notable herald) and gives him a rebated tournament sword. On this occasion René relates how the Duke of Brittany sent the Duke of Bourbon a challenge to a '*Tournoy et Bouhordis d'armes*' before ladies and girls. Four judges were to be appointed, two from the district of the defendant and two from elsewhere, all being worthy barons, knights or squires.

The *destrier* of the lord enters the town first, a small page in the saddle. The *destriers* of the other tourneying knights and squires follow in pairs. Behind come trumpeters and minstrels, then heralds, pursuivants and the tourneying knights and squires with their entourage. Four trumpeters lead the judges' procession; then come the king-of-arms, the four judges and the rest of the company.

Keeping their retinue together, the judges try to put up at a religious house, since the cloister was ideal for the display of crests the following day. The judges should have a canvas three feet by two in size, showing the banners and names of the two chief tourneyers (appellant and defendant) at the top, and at the foot the four banners with names, surnames, seigneuries, titles and offices of the four judges. On the day the banners of the princes are borne to the cloister by one of their chamberlain knights, and the pennons carried by the foremost valets or squires. The helms of princes are carried by the chief squire, those of other knights and squires by gentlemen or valets. The following day the contestants ride to the lists unarmed except for staves, with their banner bearers carrying furled banners. There, each raises his right hand and swears to obey the rules of the tournament.

## Ordinances

Contestants often set out specific rules, such as types of weapon and number of blows, in '*Chapitres d'Armes*' which might be formulated as much as a year before the actual event. A late 15th century example states that a contestant who withdraws beyond the '*barres*' may not return that day.

In England a set of ordinances was drawn up in 1466 by John Lord Tiptoft, Earl of Worcester, at the command of Edward IV. They were to be kept in all manner of jousts of peace 'royall' in England; later ordinances tend to be very similar. Surviving copies show that the prize is awarded for the following feats, in order of preference:

Unseating with the lance, or bearing horse and rider to earth.
Striking the opponent's coronel twice.
Striking the sight of the helm three times.
Correctly breaking the most spears.
Staying in the field longest and still helmed, and having run the fairest course and given the greatest strokes, best with the spear.

The tilt barrier not only prevented collisions: without it, jousters could meet head on, the full force of horse and rider being imparted to the lance tip. Over the barrier the lance must be swung to the left. It has been calculated that allowing the riders moved on a line 3 ft. from the tilt, the angle of a lance with 12 ft. projecting would be between 25 and 30 degrees. At this angle it would be much easier to break the lance.

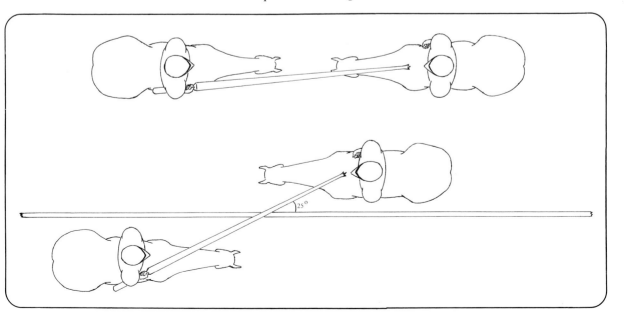

Sir Edmund Darundell is led on a golden chain by his lady. This illustration from a late 15th-century copy of the Salisbury Roll echoes a number of descriptions in which knights are led by ladies to the lists with chains. The knight wears a tight heraldic jupon over his breastplate. The barred helmet is of the style used in the club tournament. His arms are repeated on the rich dress of his wife. (By permission of the British Library.)

Prizes are lost for striking a horse, striking a man's back (turned or disarmed of his spear), hitting the tilt barrier three times, or unhelming oneself twice (unless the horse fails).

A spear is allowed for breaking a lance between saddle and the charnel (breast fixture) of the helm, or from the charnel upwards. Three spears are allowed for breaking a lance by unhorsing the opponent, or so disarming him that he cannot continue. A spear is disallowed, however, for breaking the lance on the saddle, whilst two spears are disallowed for striking the tilt and three if it happens twice. A lance which snaps within a foot of the coronel head is not considered as broken, simply a good 'attaint'.

Problems occurred which only the judges could solve. Lances and even horses must be of similar size. Jehan de Boniface was allowed a sharp lance, but not one furnished with four vicious points. Galiot de Baltasin appeared at Arras in 1446 on a horse whose chanfron and body armour were fitted with steel spikes, and was promptly told to remove them. His opponent, Philippe de Ternant, broke his sword belt in the combat so that his sword, turned in the scabbard, hung over the horse's crupper. Unable to reach it, he was forced to beat off Galiot with his hand until the sword fell out on to the sand. Only then was he considered disarmed so that his weapon could be restored to him in accordance with the 'chapitres'.

Some idea of the size of the lists may be gleaned from references to a meeting held at Smithfield in 1467. The area was 370 by 250 feet with a double palisade. Edward IV, acting as judge, sat in a stand reached by steps. Three other stands held knights, esquires and royal archers of the guard, whilst one on the opposite side housed the mayor and aldermen. Both the constable and the marshal of the lists were provided with chairs. The constable's guard of eight mounted men-at-arms took their place, together with a crowned king-of-arms and herald or pursuivant at each corner. Garter and other kings-of-arms were near Edward's right side in the stand. At St. Omer in 1446 a stone tribune had been built for the judges. At the Field of the Cloth of Gold in 1520 the arena measured 400 by 200 paces, encircled by a ditch and bank nine feet high; the lists measured 150 paces. Some references show them set east to west, perhaps to prevent the sun dazzling one of the contestants or the high lords present, since their stands seem to have been placed on the south side.

The most significant feature of the 15th century was the introduction of the tilt barrier to separate the contestants in a joust. Illustrations show that without a barrier jousters could meet their opponent on the left or right side. Not only did some deliberately 'ride down' their opponents, but collisions and close passes could cause injury to horses and severe bruising to the rider's knees. The tilt was designed to avoid this. First mentioned by Monstrelet in connection with a joust at Arras in 1429, the 'tilt' or 'toile' was initially a rope hung with cloth. The Count of St. Martin apparently preferred to ride from a corner of the lists, which proved to be his undoing: in a joust with Guillaume

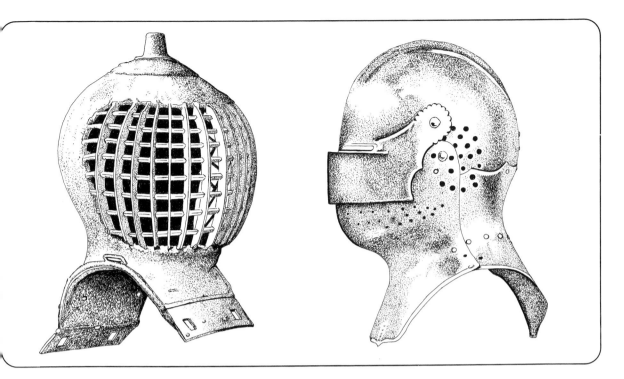

*Left:* helmet of *c.*1480 fitted with a grille, for use in the German *'Kolbenturnier'* or club tourney. *Right:* a type of German helmet evolved for combat on foot, dating from around 1500.

de Vaudray his oblique charge exposed his right arm because of a faulty piece of armour—Vaudray's lance struck this point, leaving the head embedded in the wound.

The tilt probably first appeared in Italy, since jousts using this innovation were referred to as the 'Italian Course'. It did not reach England until the 1430s, and was not popular in Germany until the end of the century. The tilt did not replace the older form of open jousting, which continued as an alternative form. It was never used in the mêlée. The rope was soon found to be inadequate, and was generally replaced by a wooden barrier up to six feet high. Sixteenth-century illustrations sometimes show the ends of the tilt bent out in such a way that at the end of the run the jouster must turn to his right; this would prevent him running on into the fences or tents beyond the tilt. Further, the other

A South German harness of about 1500 for use in the *'Scharfrennen'*. There is no armour for the limbs; the *'Renntartsche'* and the vamplate of the lance afford sufficient protection for the arms, whilst the tilting-sockets cover much of the legs. The *'volant pieces'* attached to the brow of the sallet were designed to fly off when struck. There was no barrier in this course—a 'blind' chanfron (armour for the horse's head) is provided to prevent the animal shying. (By courtesy of the Board of Trustees, Royal Armouries.)

27

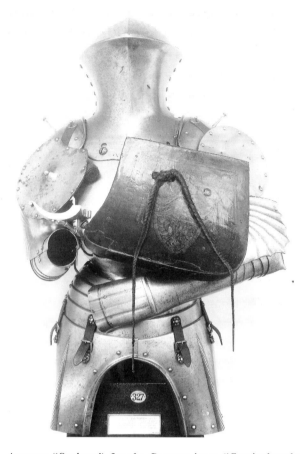

Armour ('*Stechzeug*') for the German joust ('*Gemeinedeutsche Gestech*') made at Augsburg between 1500 and 1520. The fluted frog-mouthed helm ('*Stechhelm*') is screwed down to the breastplate to save the head from being forced back if the helm should be struck. The breastplate is boxed on the right to accommodate the lance. A '*polder-mitton*' is riveted to the right forearm plate to guard the elbow bend. The right hand has no gauntlet, being protected by the large vamplate of the lance. The left hand, however, is covered by the '*manifer*'. There is no leg armour since the chest padding of the horse protected the lower limbs. The shield ('*Stechtartsche*'), of oak about 2.8cm. thick, is pierced with two holes for the plaited flaxen cord, as is the breastplate beneath. In the centre is painted a shield of arms bearing a displayed eagle within a border gobony, with a helm and peacock feather crest above. (Reproduced by permission of the Trustees of the Wallace Collection, London.)

Rear view of the same armour. The back plate is of three pieces, and the large 'queue' (*Rasthaken*) for holding the lance can be seen clearly. The buckle on the left pauldron held the strap which supported the shield. Decorative mantling from the helm was probably twisted round the projecting sprockets. The armour weighs 90 lb; falling from a horse in such a harness must have been a memorable experience . . . Several holes in the breastplate have been patched from the inside, while the surface bears evidence of marks, not from coronels as was usual in this course, but from square lance-heads. (Reproduced by permission of the Trustees of the Wallace Collection, London.)

end was effectively blocked and so forced the rider to take the right hand path.

## The Pas d'armes

Though terms such as '*tournois*', '*joûtes*' and '*pas d'armes*' were sometimes used vaguely in the Middle Ages, it is possible to distinguish the '*pas*' by certain characteristics. In concept it revolved around the idea that several challengers or '*tenans*' would elect to hold a piece of ground (the '*pas*') against all comers, knights or squires, called the '*venans*'. As in other tournaments, this entertainment (especially popular in the 15th century) might comprise not only jousting but also foot combats and a mêlée involving all the contestants from both sides. From mid-century mounted contests with the 'baston' or club might be included.

The '*pas*' mimicked the judicial duel before judges for honour, and was a re-enactment of the type of situation encountered in early epic literature. The influence of literature is especially seen in the frequent use of a '*perron*' (artificial mound or pillar) often with a 'Tree of Chivalry' nearby. It was usual to hang on the perron shields which must be touched to signify a challenge. At the Pas of Perron Fée challengers blew a horn suspended from the tree. In 1443 one such was held at the 'Tree of Charlemagne' near Dijon. The challenge was thrown out to embrace most of Christian Europe, and it was held under the eye of Philip the Good, Duke of Burgundy. Thirteen of his nobles held the '*pas*' for 40 days (excluding Sundays and feast days).

Great ingenuity went into the settings for such events. At the Pas of La Bergière in 1449 Jeanne de Laval, mistress of René of Anjou, appeared dressed as a shepherdess in a corner of lists whose galleries were thatched. Two knights representing shepherds threw down the *gage*. One bore a black shield to challenge those content in love, the other a white shield of happiness for dissatisfied amorists. That same year Jacques de Lalain held the Pas of Fontaine des Pleurs on an island in the River Saône. Before a pavilion stood models of a lady and unicorn, the latter with three tear-strewn shields about its neck. The colours of white, violet and black represented courses with axe, sword and lance respectively. Losers paid a forfeit; anyone brought to the ground by an axe must wear a gold bracelet for a year or find a lady with the key. Another unicorn made an appearance at a late 15th century '*pas*': this time the shields (one on each leg) represented the opening jousts, the tourney of 12 sword strokes, foot combat with 12 sword strokes, and the defence and attack on a mock castle using shields, swords and pikes. This occurred each afternoon from 27 November to New Year's Day, and since combat went on until 7 p.m. the lists must have been illuminated by torches. At the Pas de la Pélerine at St. Omer in 1446 two shields represented Sir Lancelot and Tristan de Leonnois.

At the Smithfield '*pas*' of 1467 a knocking at the gate signalled the entry of 'Escallis' (Lord Scales), who was followed by about 12 richly caparisoned horses led by pages. In his joust with the Bastard of Burgundy, the latter's horse struck its head against the pommel of Scales' saddle and fell with its rider. Some chroniclers assert that a spike on the chanfron of Scales' *destrier* was thrust into the mouth of the other animal; the Bastard's comment was that he had fought a beast and tomorrow would fight a man. This was done on foot; the casting spears were considered too dangerous, and combat was agreed with axes and daggers. Olivier de la Marche, who was present, testifies to the great rents made in Scales' armour by the lower point of the Bastard's axe.

At the Pas à l'Arbre d'Or in 1468 a fir tree sheathed in gold was set up opposite the ladies' stand in the market place at Bruges. The festivities marked the marriage of Charles of Burgundy with the sister of Edward IV and were to last ten days. A pursuivant handed the duke a letter from a princess who would proffer favour to any knight who would deliver a giant from captivity, whom she had placed under protection of her dwarf. The latter entered in crimson and white satin, leading the giant. Together with the pursuivant of the Toison d'Or they were to take their place by three pillars on a stage set on a perron. Cleves Pursuivant knocked on one gate of the lists with a hammer, and on admittance his coat-of-arms was hung on the tree. Adolf of Cleves, Lord of Ravestein, was conducted into the lists disguised as a very old man (popular with organisers) and asked for permission to tilt. The Bastard of Burgundy entered within a rich portable pavilion. The dwarf turned a sand glass for half an hour's duration, and blew his horn. A banquet ended the first day's events. A *destrier* was the prize, richly caparisoned and provided with panniers containing a jousting harness of the Bastard of Burgundy. Finally the tilt and stands were removed, and the mêlée took place with rebated swords. So ardent were the tourniers that

Spring mechanism made in Germany for a '*Mechanisches Rennen*' in which a shield placed on the front exploded in fragments when struck. This example was probably made for use in a '*Bundrennen*' in which no throat armour was used—a course in vogue in German lands during the early 16th century. (Waffensammlung, Vienna.)

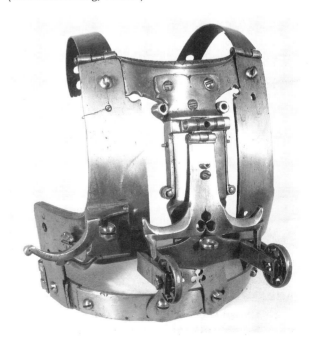

A lining for a '*Stechhelm*', *c.*1500. The wider straps were brought out at the sides and buckled behind the head, whilst the thongs were threaded through eyelets in the helm and knotted. Though capable of movement, the head was held securely in a web which cushioned the impact when struck or unhorsed. (Waffensammlung, Vienna.)

they ignored all signals to cease until the duke, bare-headed and sword in hand, pushed his way into the press.

## Foot Combat

It was the 15th century that saw the rise in popularity of foot combats. Often they were part of a general challenge in which combat took place both on horse and foot. They may derive from those contests used in the judicial duel. In the lists a number of rules were in force, though armour was at the discretion of the wearer. For much of the 15th century this meant ordinary field harness, but towards the end of the century a form with a deep skirt or 'tonlet' (which earlier had appeared briefly in Germany) was seen. The helmet was usually a bascinet, but sallets might be worn. In about 1500 a 'bellows' form of visor appeared, as well as a hemispherical style, the former remaining popular until mid-century. These were often fixed to the helmet as extra pieces.

A small religious flag was usually carried into the lists by each competitor. Often a lance or even a sword was first cast before closing to deliver a set number of blows. During a contest in the Pas de la Pélerine Jacques de Lalain's wrist was pierced and bled copiously. He fought on with his own axe tucked under his arm, grabbing at his opponent's weapon, since the Duke of Burgundy refused to stop the fight and allow his own man to lose. Lalain eventually stepped back so that his English adversary fell forward as he lunged in his heavier

The padded lining for the '*Stechhelm*' allowed for movement of the head while cushioning it in a web of straps and thongs. With this type of helmet it was possible to see the opponent by leaning forward during the charge. Just before impact the body was straightened, preventing entry of the opposing lance through the vision slit.

armour. Protests that only elbows and knees had touched earth were fruitless; the whole body was judged to have fallen. Other rules sometimes did not allow even a knee to touch. A set of English rules for 1554 specify that the prize is lost for hitting below the belt, using a locking gauntlet, dropping a sword, striking the barrier with the hand, or not showing the sword to the judges before combat.

At the end of the 15th century a barrier—often a simple bar but sometimes a planked fence—was introduced to separate the contestants. Now they could not grapple but must strike over the top of it, though there are instances of one combatant trying to pull the other over the top. One description refers to a bar at either end which could be swung across to stop the fight when the judge required it, whilst an illustration of a combat before Elizabeth I shows a mesh screen to protect the queen from flying fragments. Poleaxe, sword, axe and dagger were usual; the *Freydal* of Maximilian I illustrates combat with many other weapons, including bastard sword, mace, guisarme, '*Aalspiess*', quarterstaff and flail. During the 16th century the '*Fussturnier*' appeared, in which several contestants fought in two groups over the barrier. In this and some other courses the challengers were called '*maintenators*', their opponents '*aventuriers*'.

**Specialised Armour**

The joust was now developing gradually into several forms, run either with or without a tilt barrier. As time went on more specialised pieces were developed to be worn only during the joust, and hence these harnesses began to differ from those used for war. In England the first reference to these special armours appears to come from a bequest from Lord Bergavenny during the reign of Edward IV. In Burgundy a reference occurs for 1443. A French manuscript of 1446 notes a number of pieces for the joust, which were adopted in most countries. A helm was strapped to a brigandine or a cuirass, fitted with a lance rest. The left hand and forearm

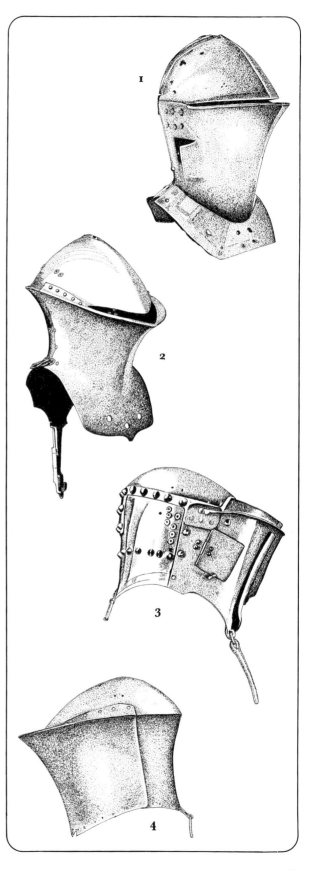

**The frog-mouthed jousting helm may show regional variations. (1) The type used in France, Flanders and England; the illustrated example has a 'chin' introduced in the second decade of the 16th century. It also has a detachable front portion, an English feature enabling the helm to convert to a bascinet for tourney or foot combat. (2) German helm with fluted decoration and sweeping lines. (3) Squat Italian helm of 'pill box' form. (4) One of a group of English helms which also display 'pill box' characteristics. All are roughly contemporary.**

were guarded by a '*manifer*'; the right hand was enclosed in a '*gaignepain*' or glove (probably of leather); the right elbow was protected by a '*polder-mitton*'; a laminated right pauldron had a large, circular '*besagew*'; a '*poire*' or pear-shaped buffer of wood was attached to the left breast behind the wooden rectangular shield. The latter was faced with square pieces of horn and attached by a cord. Leg armour was normal for jousting in France.

In England three types of course became established. The 'joust of peace' utilised a harness rather like that mentioned above. The jousters ran along the tilt, left side to left side, with coronel-headed lances. The second course, or 'joust of war', was run in field armour with sharp lances. The helmet was often an armet and wrapper. A large reinforcement for the left shoulder, the '*grandguard*,' and another for the left elbow, the '*pasguard*', were introduced in the middle of the century. The third type was the joust 'at large' or 'at random', which differed from the last only in the absence of the barrier. Once the lances had been used, the combatants removed their reinforces and took to

**Fighting with rebated swords, from the early 16th century *Tournament Book of the Duke of Bavaria*. On the right are the Dukes of Bavaria and Mecklenburg, on the left two Margraves of Brandenburg. A second sword hangs at the saddle bow, whilst reinforcing pieces used in the initial encounter with lances lie on the ground. (Bayerische Staatsbibliothek, Munich.)**

1: William Marshal, c.1170
2: Philip of Flanders, c.1181
3: Footsoldier

A

Windsor, 1278:
1: William de Valence, Earl of Pembroke
2: Pembroke's squire
3: Roger de Trumpington

B

1: Sir John Holland, 1390
2: Sir John's lady
3: Sir John's squire

C

1: King-of-Arms of Duke of Brittany, mid-15th C.
2: Pursuivant
3: Trumpeter of the Lord of Gruthuyse

D

'The Tree of Charlemagne', 1443:    1:   Herald of Pierre de Bauffrement     2:   Herald of Diago de Valiere     3:   Diago de Valiere

E

The mêlée, mid-15th C:
see text for commentaries.

F

G

Foot combat, 1446:
1: John, Bastard of St. Pol
2: Bernard, Bastard of Foix
3: Herald of the Duke of Burgundy
4: Man-at-arms

H

The Gestech, c.1500:
1: Herzog Hans zu Sachsen
2: Varlet
3: Marshal

I

Westminster Tournament, 1511:
1: King Henry VIII
2: Opponent
3: Attendants

J

'The Run of the Disappearing Shield', c.1520:
1: Emperor Maximilian I
2: Sigmund von Welsperg

K

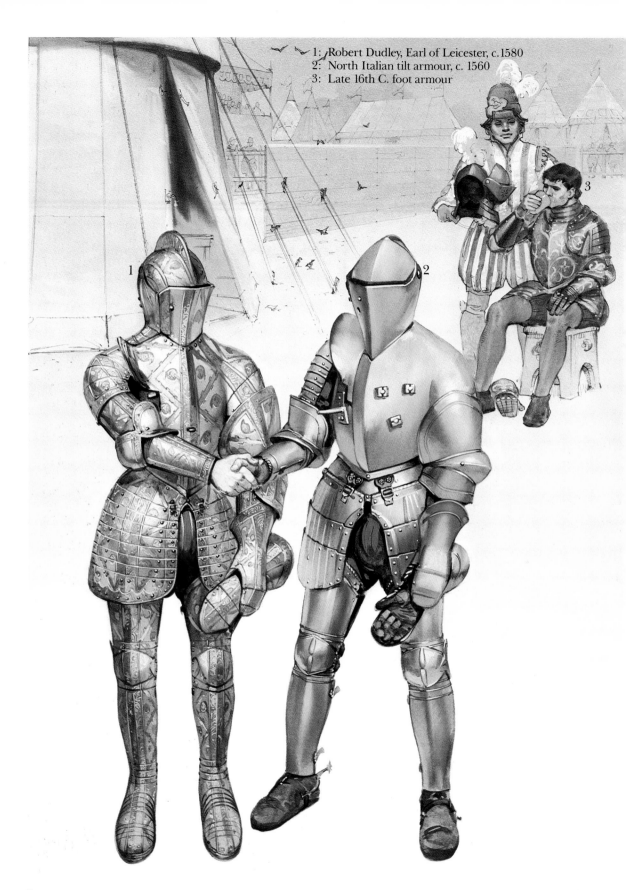

1: Robert Dudley, Earl of Leicester, c.1580
2: North Italian tilt armour, c. 1560
3: Late 16th C. foot armour

L

blunt swords. The mêlée was similar to this except that a number of riders took part.

In Germany the armour described in the French manuscript formed the basis for the course known as the 'Gestech'. Field harness with frog-mouthed 'Stechhelm' and rectangular shield were probably used, together with rebated lances. Already in 1436 an inventory of Friedrich of Tyrol mentions special pieces. Leg harness was not used, since the front of the saddle was extended to protect the lower limbs. In about 1480 this was replaced by a padded bumper or 'Stechsack' which was hung round the horse's chest in a similar way to the earlier 'hourt'. The saddle was furnished with a low cantle which would not impede unhorsing, though splintering the lance was equally desirable. In the 'Hohenzeug-gestech', however (which appeared at the end of the 14th century), the saddle tree rose some ten inches above the horse's back, so that the rider stood in the stirrups. A high cantle and additional side bars fixed him in his seat, greatly increasing the risk of a strained or broken back. This course declined after 1450 until revived briefly at the turn of the 16th century.

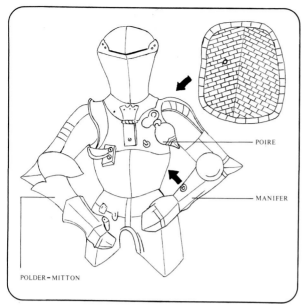

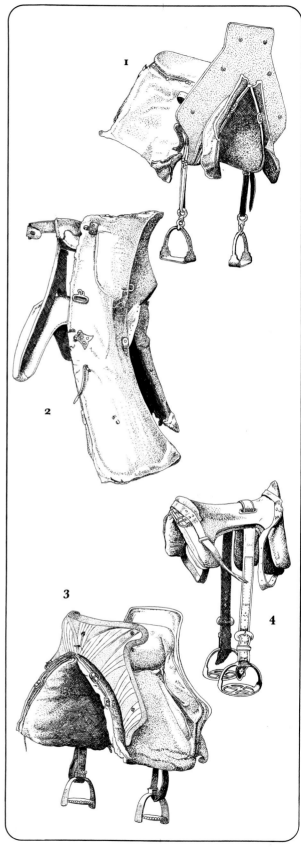

POIRE

MANIFER

POLDER-MITTON

**Special pieces of armour evolved for the joust, seen here on a Flemish harness depicted in the early 16th century *Inventario Illuminado*. The '*poire*' acted as a buffer for the shield which was attached with a cord. A feature of some Flemish jousting armours was the staple on the '*manifer*' enabling the arm to be tied up to the breast in the correct position.**

The '*Rennen*' or '*Scharfrennen*' formed the second group of German runs, from which a number of derivatives appeared. The '*Scharfrennen*' is also first mentioned in 1436. Until the last quarter of the 15th century pictorial evidence suggests that protection for this consisted of a half-armour or brigandine, with sallet and bevor to protect head and throat. A rectangular shield was used, the object being to unhorse the opponent using a sharp lance.

A form of the mêlée which appeared at this time was the '*Kolbenturnier*' or baston course: a '*Kolben*' or heavy club was used, of polygonal cut and swelling out towards an obtuse point. This spectacle probably developed from judicial foot combats for lower classes, which utilised the club. No lances were used, the object being to batter the large crests of opposing team contestants. A globose bascinet was screwed down to the cuirass, fitted with a lattice of iron bars and the whole covered with leather which could be painted. Inside it was heavily padded and roomy. High-backed saddles were used

**Surviving saddles from the early 16th century: (1) for the '*Gestech*'. (2) For the '*Hohenzeuggestech*'. A deep saddle tree was used and additional side bars (missing here) held the rider securely. (3) For jousting over the barrier and for tourney. (4) For the '*Rennen*'.**

to secure the riders in their seats. Rüxner mentions a German mêlée in the late 15th century in which clubs were used for two hours, at which time a signal was given to change to rebated swords. The 'Kolbenturnier' survived into the first quarter of the 16th century but thereafter fell out of favour. Only one English illustration portrays it.

# The 16th Century

With the death of Charles the Bold of Burgundy in 1477 the focus of the tournament shifted to the court of Maximilian I and the Holy Roman Empire. The Emperor enthusiastically promoted the sport. It is to Germany that we must turn for much information concerning the tournament in the 16th century. Thanks to the details left in the *Freydal, Der Weisskünig*, the *Triumph of Maximilian* and other German sources a tentative picture may be presented. Prizes in these contests consisted of such items as a ring, a wreath, jewel, sword, helmet or charger.

Many runs in the joust were recognised, a number being devised by the emperor. The form of some of these is unknown, but all were derived from two basic types. The first of these was the 'Gestech' or 'Stechen' described above, and now called the 'Gemeinedeutsche Gestech' or 'German Gestech'. A richly decorated trapper covered the *destrier*, which might wear leather housings underneath. The 'Stechsack' guarded the animal's breast. The saddle had no cantle. Unhorsing, or at least splintering the lance, was the object of the course.

The 'Hohenzeuggestech' enjoyed a brief revival and has been mentioned above. The 'Gestech im Beinharnisch' was the German Gestech run with leg harness; the armour on the lower limbs meant that it was more difficult for the legs to grip the horse.

The 'Welsch Gestech' or 'Italian Joust' was imported to Germany, and involved the use of the tilt barrier. At first the harness worn was similar to that in the German Joust, using a 'Stechhelm' and no leg armour, but early in the 16th century the latter became established. The shield was somewhat longer, and the use of a queue to hold the lance was discarded to allow it to be swung over the tilt more easily.

The second variety of joust was the 'Rennen', which spawned even more variations. The basic run was the 'Scharfrennen' or 'Schweifrennen' with sharp lances, the early stages of which have been discussed. By 1500 it had developed into a recognisable form. A sallet ('Rennhut') and bevor ('Bart') were worn instead of a helm; no leg armour was used, but a pair of tilting-sockets ('Dilgen') were hung one each side of the saddle to guard the thighs. A large shield ('Renntartsche') of wood and leather with iron reinforcement was both attached to the breastplate and screwed to the bevor. Pictorial variations show some versions which were designed to be struck off. A saddle with low pommel and cantle was employed since unhorsing was the main object. The lance was not as thick as that used in the 'Gestech'.

'Anzogenrennen' involved the use of a very long shield coming right down to the saddle. The screw on the bevor projected noticeably. In 'Bundrennen' the object again was unhorsing, but the rider wore no bevor behind the 'Renntartsche', only a simple metal frame. Since the shield itself could be knocked off there was a danger that the lance would pierce the face. In 'Wulstrennen' no helmet was used; the 'Renntartsche' was high and provided with an eye slit. 'Pfannenrennen' or pan jousting employed a plate which was attached to the chest. Since this course was run with no body armour at all it was highly dangerous, and a coffin was placed in the lists!

A mechanical shield was used in 'Geschift-tartscherennen': when struck, a spring triggered a mechanism which flung up the 'Renntartsche', the front face of which dissolved in wedge-shaped fragments. In 'Geschiftscheibenrennen' a large plate or disc was fixed to the chest and similarly erupted. *The Triumph of Maximilian* seems to show the same mechanism used in 'Bundrennen' and in 'Scharfrennen' when a removeable shield was employed. In both types of 'Geschiftrennen' field harness was worn. Leg armour was often added, in which case the tilting cuisses were removed.

'Feldrennen' was conducted in field armour and the saddle was fitted with a cantle; the main aim was to splinter the lance. In 'Welschrennen' a close helmet replaced the sallet and bevor, and a shield with central disc was attached to the chest. 'Kronelrennen' was probably introduced by Maximilian; one jouster was dressed for the 'Gestech', the other for the 'Scharfrennen'; the former carried a sharp lance, the latter had one with a coronel head.

The mêlée was run in field harness and the saddle had a cantle. Lance and sword were employed. The 'Feldturnier' was one form, illustrated in the Duke of Bavaria's tournament book, where reinforcing pieces are worn. Here a spare sword hangs from the saddle.

These courses remained in favour until about 1540. By then complete harnesses were being made which utilised extra 'pieces of exchange' for the tilt and tournament. This meant that in some cases one armour could be adapted appropriately for tilting or for fighting on foot, as well as for war. From about 1540 the 'Welsch Gestech' developed into the 'Plankengestech', in which a metal shield (the 'manteau d'armes') was screwed to the left shoulder and chest. This form was the last to survive, disappearing in the 17th century. The 'Gestech' itself developed in the second half of the 16th century into the 'Freiturnier', run without a tilt. The 'pasguard' on the

**Jousters in Hans Burgkmair's woodcut copy of the early 16th century *Triumph of Maximilian*. All are dressed for versions of the 'Rennen'. (1) *Pfannenrennen*; (2) '*Wulstrennen*'; (3) '*Bundrennen*'. The small projection on the chin frame is a rolling ball to allow the Remtartsche to slide over the frame. This roller can sometimes be found on surviving sallets. The other illustrations portray two of the courses run in field armour; (4) '*Geschiftscheibenrennen*'; (5) '*Welschrennen*'. (Reproduced by courtesy of the Trustees of the British Museum.)**

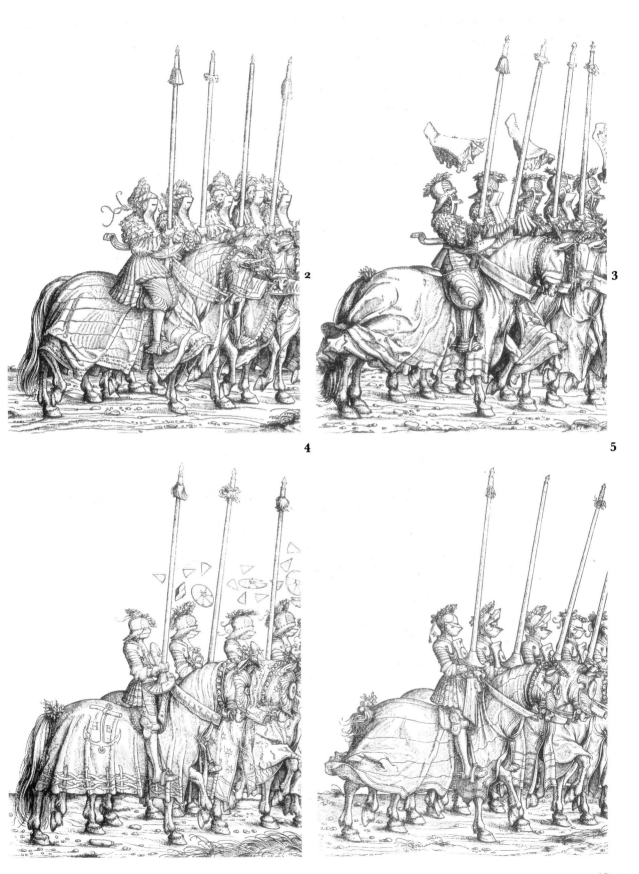

2

3

4

5

left arm was much larger than before, nearly reaching the left shoulder.

In Western Europe the form of tilting over the barrier remained the most popular throughout the 15th and 16th centuries. In 1501 a challenge mentions tilting, running with sharp weapons 'at large' (with no barrier), tourneying with swords, and foot combat with spears over a barrier. At Lille in 1513 jousts were held in a hall, the horses' hooves being shod with felt to prevent slipping on the marble floor. Except for running at large, the courses mentioned above were common in Tudor courts, the most popular being tilting or 'Jousts Royal'. The '*bourdonass*' was a hollow lance employed in tilting; surviving examples average about 12ft. in length and are fluted. Athletic exhibitions now appeared more frequently at tournaments. In 1507 archery (using both standard and flight arrows), wrestling and casting the bar were included.

James IV of Scotland held some spectacular events in the style of the earlier Burgundian court, whilst Henry VIII was an enthusiast who participated in a number of elaborate tournaments.

The Westminster Tournament roll depicts the celebrations marking the birth of a son to Katherine of Aragon in 1510/11. Here 'Joyeulx Penser' (Sir Edward Neville) arrives in full armour as part of Henry VIII's team of Challengers. He is partly enclosed beneath a portable pavilion; the legs of the servant carrying the tent pole can be seen under the horse's body. Heralds ride in front. (College of Arms.)

In 1511 a mobile 'pageant' 26 ft. long entered the lists at Westminster. It was shaped like a forest complete with trees, birds, animals, foresters and a maiden. It was drawn by a gold lion and silver antelope ridden by ladies, the whole led by wildmen. Inside rode the king and three challengers, their shields fixed to the four corners of the forest. The war with France between 1512 and 1514 seems to have curtailed such lavish displays thereafter.

An exception was the meeting with Francis I at the Field of the Cloth of Gold in 1520 for which a huge Tree of Honour was constructed. Rain and wind adversely affected the tilting, and Henry insisted on the removal of the counterlists, which caused the horses to swerve. Costumes were sumptuous: one was covered with separate branches and leaves, all made in gold.

In 1524/5 Henry took part in Christmas tilting, tourneying and barriers before the 'Castle of Loyaltie'. Nearby was a mound with unicorn and shields; the defences were manned by a captain and 15 gentlemen. The castle, in Greenwich tiltyard, rose 50ft. high and was 20ft. square, being reinforced with iron. Four knights attacked two defenders using pike, target and rebated sword. Unfortunately tempers frayed during the second attack on the day following, and the proceedings declined into a stone-throwing contest.

These mock assaults on sham castles had been

popular early in the reign; but on the Continent such attacks were carried out with much more violence. A variation of the '*pas*', the '*Scharmützel*' involved a castle, gate, or bridge-head of wood constructed to form the centre of a miniature siege. In 1507 an attack on a castle watched by Louis XII caused the death of one contestant. Francis I ordered a miniature wooden town with ditches, 100 cavalry and 400 infantry at celebrations for the marriage of the Duke of Urbino in 1517. It lasted a month, and included cannon firing hollow balls. At Dresden in 1553 four troops of cavalry attacked a castle whose garrison were armed with military forks, '*Aalspiesse*' (pikes) and 400 earthenware pots to throw. Cannon were used by both sides.

## Demise and Revival

The tournament never totally lost its element of danger. An attack on a pageant ship in Rome (1501) injured five combatants. As in Germany, some other areas (Trani and Valladolid, for example) still included courses with sharp lances. Occasionally—even in the mid-17th century—jousts were run without a tilt barrier, as in Danzig. Despite armour specifically designed to lessen the risk of injury, accidents could and did happen. In March 1524 the Duke of Suffolk nearly killed Henry VIII: in shivering his lance on the monarch's helmet the visor was flung back and the headpiece filled with splinters. Luckily for Suffolk the king was

unhurt and apparently unruffled. Henri II of France was less fortunate: he insisted on breaking an extra lance with the Constable de Montgomeri during a joust in 1559. The latter shattered his lance, but did not drop it immediately, and a splinter entered the king's visor, fatally wounding him. After this the tournament never regained its popularity.

Knights still tilted, tourneyed and fought at barriers, however: James I participated in the Accession Day tilts of 1612, and seven years later his son Charles, Prince of Wales, processed to the tiltyard at Whitehall in armour, mounted on a richly caparisoned and plumed charger. Lances had become more fragile so that they might shatter easily. In some parts of Europe forms of the tournament survived until the early 18th century.

The '*pas d'armes*' was transformed into the Elizabethan Triumph with emphasis on masques. The '*Carrousel*' or '*Karoussel*' then appeared, and was much favoured at the court of Louis XIV: two teams of horsemen were provided with shields and bombarded each other with hollow clay balls which might be filled with powder or scented water. Sometimes padded clubs or blunt swords were used to demolish the crests of the other team, but the

*Left:* **a close helmet for the '*Welschrennen*', probably made at Augsburg *c*.1500.** *Right:* **a German tilting helmet *c*.1580. The small cord released the upper visor, a small 'door' in the side of the helmet provided ventilation.**

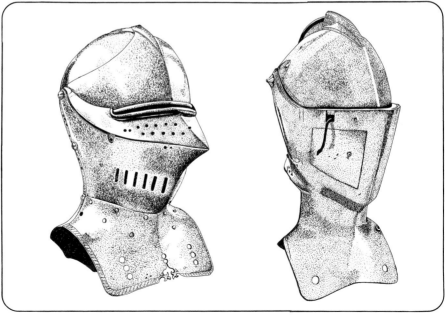

armour used here was largely of gilded copper or thin iron plate. Knights still rode at the quintain and the ring, or speared dummy 'Saracens' heads'. The pageantry was as gaudy as ever, but in the 17th century skill with the lance was being replaced by that of horsemanship. Riding masters such as Antoine de Pluvinel taught the art of the '*maneige*', of how to handle not warhorses, but Neapolitans or barbs.

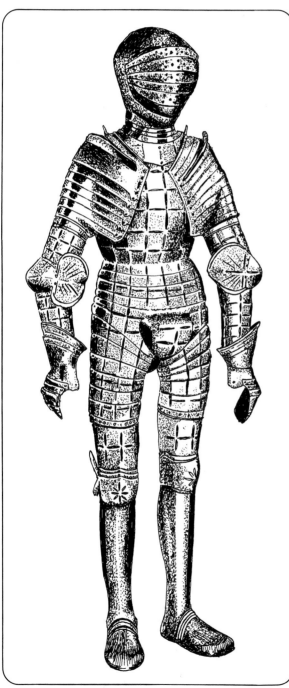

Attempts to revive the medieval tournament were made in the 19th century, the most notable instance being the Eglington Tournament of 1839 organised by the 13th Earl. In a familiar story, much of the expensive preparations fell victim to the English weather. More recently several groups of modern 'knights' have begun to organise regular tournaments which entertain large numbers of people. Despite its violence the tournament had served a purpose: to nurture the ideals of chivalry and to disseminate them via the multitudes who flocked to these displays.

## Further Reading

Anglo, Sidney, 'Score Cheques and Lists' in *Journal of the Society of Archivists*, Vol II no. 4, 1961
—— *The Great Tournament Roll of Westminster*, 1968
Anjou, René d', *Traité de la Forme et Devis d'un Tournoi*, ed. Revue Verve Paris, Vol IV, 1946
Barber, Richard, *The Knight and Chivalry*, 1970
Blair, Claude, *European Armour*, 1958
Clephan, R. Coltman, *The Tournament, its Periods and Phases*, 1919
Cline, Ruth, 'The Influence of Romance on the Tournaments of the Middle Ages' in *Speculum XX*, 1945 pp204–11
Cripps-Day, Francis, *The History of the Tournament in England and in France*, 1918
Denholm-Young, N., 'The Tournament in the 13th century' in *Studies in Medieval History presented to F. M. Powicke*, 1948 pp240–68
Duvernoy, Emile & Harmand, René, *Le Tournoi de Chauvency en 1285*, 1905
Dillon, Viscount, 'Tilting in Tudor Times' in *Archaeological Journal LV* pp296–321, 329–39
—— 'Barriers and Foot Combats' in *Archaeological Journal LXI*, pp276–308
Gamber, Ortwin, 'Die Harnischgarnitur' in *Livrustkammaren* Vol 7, 1955, pp45–114
—— 'Der Turnierharnisch zur zeit König Maximilians I und das Thunsche Shizzenbuch' in *Jahrbuch der Kunsthistorischen Sammlungen in Wien 53* (XVII), 1957, pp33–70
Gamber, Ortwin & Thomas, Bruno, *Katalog der Leibrüstkammer, Vol I*, 1976 Kunsthistorisches Museum, Wien, Waffensammlung

**Milanese armour of the early 16th century. Made for foot combat, it completely envelops the wearer in metal, yet mimics the puffs and slashes of civilian costume.**

Haenel, Erich, *Der Sächsischen Kürfursten Turnier-bücher*, 1910

Keen, Maurice, *Chivalry*, 1984

Martin, Paul, *Armour and Weapons*, 1967

Meyer, P. (ed.), *L'histoire de Guillaume le Maréchal, Comte de Striguel et de Pembroke*, 1891–1901

Niedner, Felix, *Das Deutsche Turnier im XII und XIII Jahrhundert*, 1881

Norman, A.V.B. and Pottinger, Don, *Warrior to Soldier 449–1660*, 1966

Reitzenstein, Alexander Freiherr von, *Rittertum und Ritterschaft*, 1972

Young, Alan *Tudor and Jacobean Tournaments*, 1987

# The Plates

*A1: William Marshal participating at a tournament in France, c.1170*

Basic protection comes from a mail hauberk, here provided with mufflers which leave the fingers free. He wears a long surcoat, the colours of which do not reflect those of his arms. The reconstruction is only partially based on his effigy in the Temple Church, London, since this is probably a product of the mid-13th century. He bears the arms of the office of Marshal of England.

*A2: Philip, Count of Flanders, from his seal of c.1181*

In tournaments the Count would lurk on the sidelines, then rush in when everyone was exhausted. William Marshal pretended not to be involved at all until the Count had committed himself: only then did he attack the Flemings. Philip wears the new cylindrical form of helmet, here provided with tails like a bishop's mitre; though originally ties for securing headwear, their position suggests that they were now worn as badges of rank. His shield is very modern and carries the lion of Flanders, which is also painted on his helmet. His earlier seal shows a more rounded top edge, whilst the left side depicts a lion rampant facing the centre as if confronting a second beast on the hidden side.

**Foot combat armour of Henry VIII. This is probably the armour made at Greenwich for the Field of the Cloth of Gold in 1520, but discarded when the specifications for such combat were altered. It offers complete protection, being provided with steel breeches and codpiece, pauldrons which cover the armpits and laminated strips at elbow and knee joints. When closed the fingers of the right gauntlet may be locked to ensure a weapon is not lost. (By courtesy of the Board of Trustees, Royal Armouries.)**

*A3: Footsoldier*

At this time it was acceptable for footsoldiers to be utilised in beating off opposing knights. This man wears a kettle hat and padded 'aketon'.

*B: The Windsor Tournament, 1278:*
*B1: William de Valence, Earl of Pembroke*

The Purchase Roll of items for this affair allows a

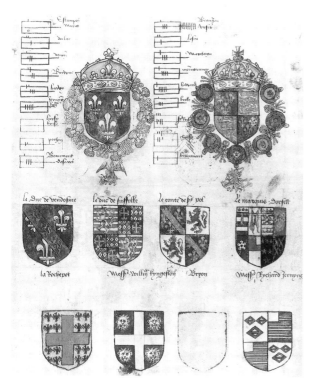

**The arms of participants in the jousting at the Field of the Cloth of Gold, 1520. Next to the royal arms of Francis I of France and Henry VIII of England are the scores recorded in one of the contests. (Society of Antiquaries, London.)**

tentative reconstruction to be made. The earl wears a cindon silk surcoat over a cuirass of gilt leather with buckram sleeves. His legs are unprotected. A gilt helm of *cuir bouilli* carries a fan crest, also borne by his charger. '*Aillettes*' on the shoulders are tied with silken cords and repeat his arms: made from leather and corda, it is likely they were used for display rather than protection. The sword is of whalebone covered in parchment and silvered. The hilt has been gilded. As a novice De Valence took part in his first tourney in 1248, and was beaten up for his pains.

### B2: Squire to the Earl of Pembroke

Bearing the device of his lord, he is dressed according to the instructions given in perhaps the earliest version of the *Statuta de Armorum* which may date to 1267. Here the squire is unarmoured except for quilted thigh defences ('*quisers*') and solid shin pieces ('*mustiliers*'). Banner bearers were allowed cane shoulder pieces as well, and a perhaps slightly later version mentions helmets ('*bacyns*') as well. Such rules are likely to have been observed in this tourney, since William de Valence was one of those who petitioned the king to confirm them. Their necessity strongly suggests that many came heavily armoured and bristling with weapons.

### B3: Roger de Trumpington

Based partly on his effigy at Trumpington in Cambridge (though this may date to the 14th century), his armour is similar to that of the other contestants. However, unlike the '*digniores*', his helm is only silvered. The chain to stop the sword being lost is mentioned in the contemporary Chauvency tournament. No reference to lances is made in the Purchase Roll.

### C1: Sir John Holland, Smithfield Tournament, 1390

After descriptions in Froissart and Caxton: by now much of the body was protected by plates, and a tight '*jupon*' often covered the torso. Underneath, a leather coat with iron plates attached is worn over a hauberk and padded '*aketon*'. The armour is basically that used in warfare, with slight modifications for the tourney field, such as a heavy steel gauntlet for the left hand; called a '*manifer*' (literally 'hand of iron') its form at this date is speculative. Sir John's badge of a white hart shows him to be one of King Richard II's party of challengers.

### C2: Lady

She also displays the white hart badge. Caxton relates that this was worn everywhere by the king's party, while accounts for another royal tourney the following year include rolls of green cloth. The lady leads her knight by a chain at the head of 60 such couples (or 24 according to Froissart). Over her kirtle she wears a sideless surcoat, cut low over the hips to reveal the 'knightly girdle'.

### C3: Squire

He rides his master's great horse or '*destrier*', and brings up the rear of the procession of warhorses. The *destrier* is said to have been so-called because it was trained to lead with the 'dexter'—or right—leg. This young man, about 20 years old, wears the latest fashion: a short '*houppelande*' or gown with

**A model of a jouster made in about 1540. The armour is that for the '*Gestech*', and the horse furniture carries the arms of the Holzschuher family from Nuremberg. (Bayerisches Nationale Museum, Munich.)**

54

high neck and dagged edging. Sir John's crested great helm has a reinforcing plate on the left side.

### D1: King-of-arms
Taken from the mid-15th century tournament book of King René of Anjou. The ermine on his loose tabard marks him as the representative of the Duke of Brittany. On his left shoulder he wears a rich embroidered satin cloth to which is affixed a parchment displaying the two chief contestants (appellant and defendant) in the forthcoming event. At the four corners are the arms of the judges, those of knightly rank at the top, the esquires at the bottom.

### D2: Pursuivant
He is crying the jousts, and is distinguished by his tabard, which is worn sideways (a device not used in Germany). We are told he must have a high voice! The tourney was proclaimed at the court of the appellant (challenger), then the defendant, then that of the king and finally at other courts as advised by the judges. Another pursuivant hands out little shields bearing the judges' arms to those wishing to take part in the combat.

### D3: Trumpeter
This man is from the retinue of the Lord of Gruthuyse in the Low Countries. His master's arms are displayed on the instrument. He wears breast and back plates over mail, with a cut-away jacket

**Scoring cheques recorded a contestant's ability in the lists. Those surviving date to the 16th century or later. The interpretations below are based on the observations of Sidney Anglo. At the Westminster Tournament of 1511, 264 runs were made at the tilt but only 129 attaints achieved. For the tourney with swords a simpler cheque was used; if a gauntlet was struck off this too was recorded.**

over all. His helmet is a sallet with reinforcing brow piece. A 'baselard' dagger is also carried.

### E: The Tree of Charlemagne, 1443
### E1: Herald
The Tree of Charlemagne stood on the road to Dijon. Here, in July 1443, Pierre de Bauffrement, Lord of Charny, began his 40 day ordeal to hold the 'pas' with 12 others. His arms were displayed on a tapestry before the tree. Those requiring to fight were to present themselves before the heralds. One is seen here, noting down the challenger's name.

### E2: Herald of Diago de Valiere
He touches the black shield to demonstrate that his master wishes to joust. The violet shield represented foot combat. The herald carries a spur which he will leave in token of the knight's desire to fight. It was up to the challengers to decide who would oppose De Valiere in the lists. The combat took place several days later. In one joust Jacques de Challant so damaged the arm-guard of De Valiere that a three-hour delay occurred while it was repaired.

### E3: The Castilian knight, Diago de Valiere
Such theatre was commonplace; at the Pas à L'Arbre d'Or the Lord de Ravestein was also carried into the lists in a litter.

### F/G: The Mêlée:
A mêlée in the mid-15th century, based on the tournament book of René of Anjou. The latter favoured this type of contest in which no lances were used. Tourneyers participating now often numbered perhaps 20 on each side.

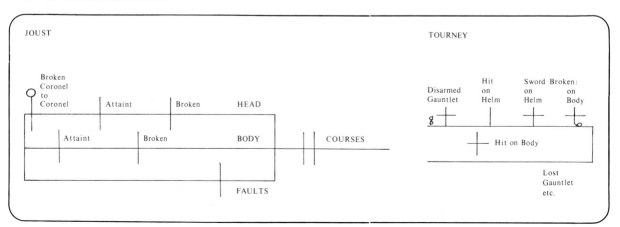

### F/G1: The Duke of Bourbon

Dressed for the club tournament, he carries a baston and a blunt sword, both of which are attached by cords. Antoine de la Sale mentions how a large millstone was set up to rebate weapons. The Duke wears limb armour of *cuir bouilli* with a heraldic tabard, and a bascinet fitted with a grille for this type of combat. His crest forms the main target.

### F/G2: The knight of honour

Picked the previous evening by two of the most beautiful ladies, he carries the 'kerchief of plaisance', embroidered, garnished and spangled with gold, on the end of a lance. Should he see any combatant in danger he will lower the kerchief over him to signify that no attack may be made. His own crested helm is held aloft in the ladies' stand.

### F/G3: Disgraced knight

He has been beaten, and forced to sit in his saddle on the palisade throughout the mêlée. De la Sale and Georges Rüxner also mention such crimes as perjury, murder, treason and abduction or dishonour of women as worthy of this punishment.

**The death of Henri II of France in 1559, in an engraving made by Perrissin in 1570 using eye witness accounts. A splinter of wood from his opponent's lance has entered the king's visor (left). Notice also the mounting steps at each end where the attendants wait with fresh weapons. De Pluvinel maintained that an armourer should always be close by, if not on the steps themselves. (Reproduced by courtesy of the Trustees of the British Museum.)**

Slander against women merited a thrashing in the lists.

### F/G4: Banner-bearer

These were not allowed to participate in the fighting, and to protect them against chance injury they wore plate armour with a variety of headgear. This man has a visored sallet. René notes that in high Germany and on the Rhine the banner-bearers were similarly dressed, with 'crayfish' or white harness, well-plumed sallets or war hats, and jackets with gold or silver thread or else their master's arms. Their horses were almost as tall as the *destriers*, and well caparisoned. He complains that in Flanders, Brabant and even in France heralds or pursuivants might be given habergeon, sallet, arm- and leg-pieces, and be forced to carry the banner on a great caparisoned horse. This so

57

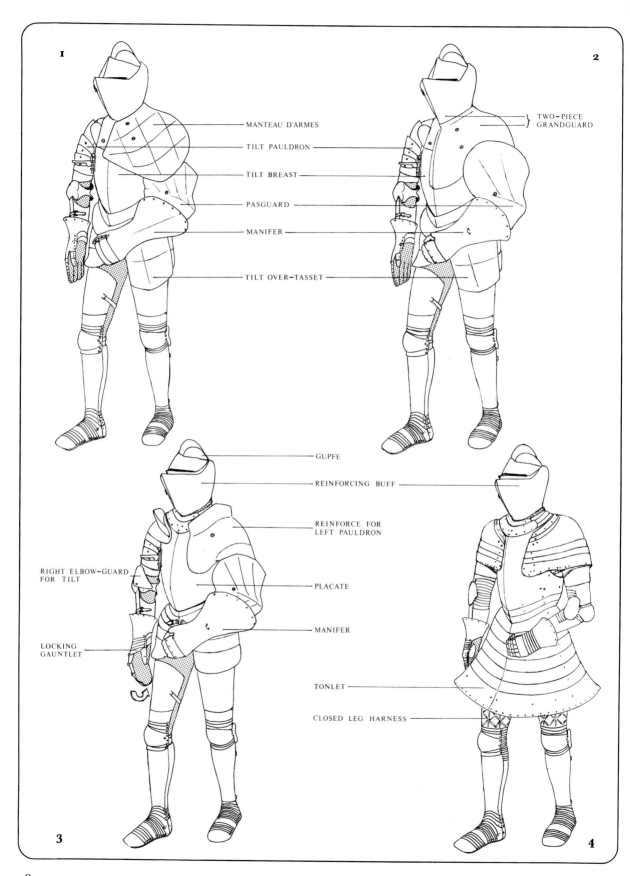

I

MANTEAU D'ARMES

TILT PAULDRON

TILT BREAST

PASGUARD

MANIFER

TILT OVER-TASSET

2

TWO-PIECE
GRANDGUARD

GUPFE

REINFORCING BUFF

REINFORCE FOR
LEFT PAULDRON

RIGHT ELBOW-GUARD
FOR TILT

PLACATE

MANIFER

LOCKING
GAUNTLET

TONLET

CLOSED LEG HARNESS

3

4

distracted them that they often dropped the banner or failed to follow their master.

## F/G5: Mounted varlet

Such men wore jasseraint or brigandine, sallet, gauntlets and leg armour. His baton is to turn blows coming towards him, and his task is to pull his master clear of the press when necessary, and to call his warcry.

## F/G6: Foot varlet

According to René he should wear a '*pourpoint*' or jacket, sallet and gauntlets, though the latter are not shown in the illustrations accompanying his text. Until needed these men waited in the space between the two rows of palisades, together with heralds, pursuivants, trumpeters (who do not play during the combat except to signal the end of the contest) and those keeping the spectators away from the tourneyers. Unable to raise up their master, the varlets must protect him with their staves until the end of the combat. They might then expect a reward of wine.

## F/G7: Judge

Marked out by his white stave of office, he is dressed in a long '*houppelande*'. His arms and those of his companions are displayed below. He would share the stand with the king-of-arms, who would be ready to provide information about the contestants. A later 15th century reference mentions a stake fixed either side of the lists with two kings-of-arms by each with pens, ink and paper to note the names of those who yielded so they could not rejoin the fray. Below the stand two ropes were stretched across the lists to separate the teams before the onset; the judges instructed the king-of-arms, who then cried '*Coupez cordes!*' three times, at which signal four men sitting on the palisades severed the ropes with axes to begin the mêlée. Another signal to commence was '*Laissez aler!*', whilst '*Holà!*' stopped the combat. The traditional cries to end the tourney were '*a l'ostel!*' or '*a logis, ployez les banniers!*'

**Garnitures allowed harness to be made up for several types of combat. This German example of about 1540 is shown in the forms for: (1) the *Plankengestech*; (2) the tilt; (3) the *Freiturnier*; the '*Gupfe*' was a reinforce for the skull of the helmet; (4) the *Fusskampf* or foot combat. The locking gauntlet, prohibited in many earlier tourneys, could be secured when the fist was closed to prevent a weapon from being dropped.**

**Armour for the '*neue welsche Gestech über die Planke*' or '*Plankengestech*'. Made at Augsburg in about 1590, this form of armour is distinguished by the addition of a '*manteau d'armes*' screwed to the bevor. As here, most were embossed with a trellis to allow a lance to make purchase. The left gauntlet does not belong. (Reproduced by permission of the Trustees of the Wallace Collection, London.)**

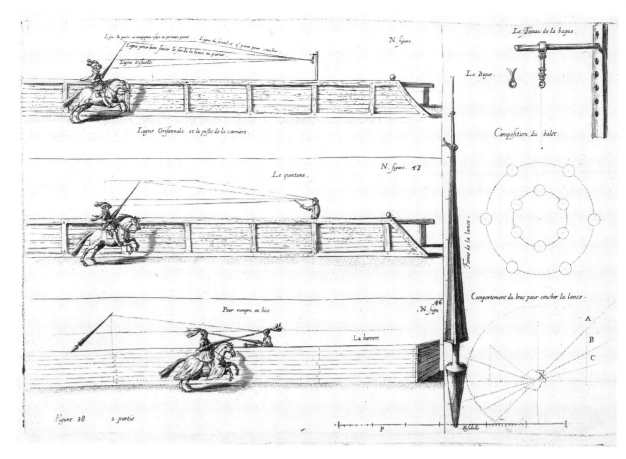

An illustration by Crispian de Pas for Antoine Pluvinel's *Maneige Royal* of 1623. From top to bottom: running at the ring; tilting at the quintain; tilting over the barrier. The spring clip which held the ring can be seen on the right. When struck correctly it was carried off on the lance. (Reproduced by courtesy of the Trustees of the British Museum.)

('to the lodging, fold banners'); René has '*Chevauchez banniers!*' ('ride on', i.e. out of the lists).

### H: Foot Combat, 1446:

**H1 and H2:** The foot combat between John, Lord of Haubourdin, Bastard of St. Pol (H1), and Bernard de Bearn, Bastard of Foix (H2), held during the 'Pas de la Pélerine' near St. Omer in 1446. John, on the left, first threw a casting spear but missed. Bernard's weapon, however, glanced off his opponent's shield and wounded him in the arm. Having hurled their shields at each other they closed for combat with the '*bec de faucon*'. Since Bernard's was fitted with a thin spike, John removed the visor from his great bascinet before combat, because his eyeslits could be penetrated easily. When they become locked together, John tried to hit his opponent on the foot.

**H3:** A herald of the Duke of Burgundy steps in at his lord's request to stop the fight. He carries a rope with knots at intervals of two feet to measure the distance a combatant should step back when requested. Though not mentioned specifically in this contest, Olivier de la Marche recalls its use in another contemporary Burgundian foot combat.

**H4:** Fully armed men-at-arms were used to force apart excited fighters when so requested; often eight such figures were stationed within the arena. This man wears an Italian harness, though brigandines might also be seen. One English manuscript shows the guards carrying halberds.

### I1: Herzog Hans zu Sachsen, c.1500

He is about to enter the lists to partake in the German '*Gestech*'. He wears armour made for this course: a 'frog-mouthed' helm, a large '*manifer*' on the left arm, and a '*polder-mitton*' on the right. His right hand is protected by the large metal vamplate on the lance. The padded '*Stechsack*' worn by his horse also guards his unarmoured legs, a necessity

Figure. 46. BBB. 2 part.

since this course was run without a barrier. As seen here, heraldic arms were not always worn in the lists; religious, political or humorous subjects were popular. As was often the case, the horse's eyes are covered. The lance is fitted with a coronel head, and the low saddle cantle does not obstruct unhorsing.

### I2: Varlet
Wearing the extravagant clothing of the day, a mounted varlet assists in leading his master to the lists. Illustrations show such men supporting the lance while it was lowered into position in the rest and under the 'queue' which juts out behind the jouster.

### I3: Marshal
The marshal and constable were the officials in charge of the lists. This figure, together with a herald, appears in several illustrations of various German courses in the *Theuerdank* of Maximilian I.

### J: The Westminster Tournament, January 1511:
Henry VIII (J1) tilting before his queen, Katherine

**Louis XIII of France jousting, from the *Maneige Royal*. Notice the hollow, fluted lance which was designed to break easily. (Reproduced by courtesy of the Trustees of the British Museum.)**

of Aragon. Notice the high wooden tilt which separates the riders. The king, as 'Coeur Loyall', wears Flemish armour, as does his opponent (J2). A veil hangs from his helm; on another occasion it bore a lady's sleeve. The decorative cloth skirts are called '*bases*'. It has been suggested that Henry's continuous success in the lists was partly due to the queen, who could stop the contest if it started to go against her husband. The illustration in the Westminster Tournament Roll on which this scene is based depicts Henry splintering his lance on the helm of his opponent. However, the surviving score cheque reveals that in reality he did not manage this feat. The Roll also shows the attendants (J3) in yellow and grey, but a comment by an early observer of the manuscript suggests that the latter colour originally appeared violet. Tilting over a barrier was especially popular in England.

Saxon armour of about 1580. A feature of harnesses from this area is the reinforcing bar connecting the helmet to the backplate.

### K1: Emperor Maximilian I, c.1520

The Emperor is shown participating in the 'Geschifttartscherennen'. This spectacular course, that of 'the Disappearing Shield', was one of the novelty runs which Maximilian popularised for a time. The right hand was protected by the large vamplate of the lance. He wears no leg armour, relying on tilting-sockets which hang from the saddle. His shoes are well wadded with tow. In some illustrations leg armour is employed in this course, in which case the 'Dilgen' would be removed. On impact the lance was dropped immediately, the raised hand denoting that this had been done.

### K2: Sigmund von Welsperg

Having been correctly struck, a spring mechanism flings up the shield, at the same time releasing the segments attached to the front face. Surviving breastplates of this kind and illustrations in German sources suggest that several types of mechanism were known. It was difficult to maintain the seat in the very low saddle; illustrations often show jousters frantically gripping the reins.

### L1: Robert Dudley, Earl of Leicester c.1580

His gilded Greenwich armour is decorated with his emblem of the ragged staff, and is fitted with tilt pieces: 'grandguard', 'pasguard' and 'manifer'. Shaking hands after a contest appears to have been expected, and is mentioned during the first half of the 15th century.

### L2: North Italian tilt armour, c.1560

The grandguard has a separate buff to protect the throat. Holes cut in the lower part of the buff accommodate two of the breastplate bolts, whilst the upper part is fixed to the close helmet. The feet are unarmoured since the jouster would be protected by iron boot stirrups. The overall appearance is plain and functional.

### L3: Late 16th century foot combat armour

The armour is blued and richly gilded. Since such contests now took place over a barrier, leg armour has been discarded. Like the other armours shown here, the visor is provided with breathing holes on the right side only; it is closed with a spring catch and wing screw.

## Notes sur les planches en couleur

**A1** Reconstitué partiellement à partir d'une effigie du treizième siècle. Remarquer que les couleurs du surcot ne correspondent pas à celles du blason du Maréchal d'Angleterre. **A2** Nouvelle forme cylindrique de heaume et bouclier très moderne décorés du lien des Flandres. **A3** A cette date, les fantassins étaient autorisés à jouer un rôle actif. Celui-ci porte le '*kettle hat*' traditionnel et un *aketon* rembourré.

**B1** Surcot de soie porté par-dessus une armure de cuir doré, et épée dorée et argentée en fanon de baleien et parchemin; à noter les armoiries sur les aillettes. **B2** Cet écuyer porte l'emblème de son seigneur; il n'a pas d'armure à l'exception de cuissardes rembourrées et de solides jambières. Les porte-étendards commençaient peut-être tout juste à porter des casques à cette époque. **B3** Basé sur cette effigie connue; l'armure est semblable à celle des autres, mais le haume est simplement argonté; le document que nous possédons ne fait pas mention de lances, mais il existe des descriptions contemporaines d'épées à chaînes.

**C1** Une bonne partie du corps est protégée par une armure constitutée de plaques; un jupon étroit recouvre un manteau en cuir assorti de plaques de fer, par-dessus in *hauberk* et un *aketon*. Cette tenue ne diffère guère de l'armure guerrière; à noter pourtant le lourd gantelet *manifer* à la main gauche. L'insigne blanche représentant un cerf blanc indique que ce personnage fait partie des provocateurs de Richard II. **C2** Cette dame conduit son chevalier par une chaîne, comme le font d'autres couples derrière eux; elle porte elle aussi les couleurs et l'insigne du roi. **C3** Cet écuyer monte le cheval de son maître et ferme la procession d'autres *destriers*. Noter que le côté gauche du heaume de Sir John est renforcé d'une plaque. Le jeune homme est habillé à la dernière mode puisqu'il porte une houppelande avec un haut col et un rebord dentelé.

**D1** Cette illustration, comme de nombreuses autres, provient du Livre de René d'Anjou. L'hermine figurant sur son tabard fait référence à la Bretagne; le parchemin placé sur son épaule gauche montre les armes des deux principaux adversaires et des juges. **D2** Ce personnage se caractérise par la manière dont il porte son tabard. Il annonce le tournoi cependant que l'on remet de petits boucliers portant les armes des juges aux futurs adversaires. **D3** Ce trompette porte les armes de son maître, le seigneur de Gruthuyse; à noter l'importante protection de son armure, et la dague *baselard*.

**E1** Les armes du seigneur de Charny figurent sur la tapisserie; ceux qui relèvent le défi et s'apprêtent à combattre donnent leur nom aux hérauts. **E2** Il s'agit ici du héraut de Diago de Valiere, qui touche le bouclier noir pour indiquer que son maître combattra à cheval; le bouclier violet symbolisait le combat au sol. L'éperon est tendu comme garant du désir de combattre. **E3** De Valiere, chevalier de Castille, observe la scène depuis sa litière; il porte son armure complète. Ces mises en scène théâtrales étaient courantes.

**F/G** La mêlée (milieu du quinzième siècle), d'après des planches détaillées du Livre de René d'Anjou. On n'utilisait pas de lances dans un combat où figuraient une vingtaine d'hommes de chaque côté. **F/G1** Le duc de Bourbon est habillé pour le combat à la massue; il est armée d'un *baston* et d'une épée émoussée attachés par des cordes et porte une armure de cuir ainsi qu'un casque à grille particulier à ce type de combat. **F/G2** Le 'chevalier d'honneur', choisi par les plus belles dames, porte un fichu brodé au bout de sa lance, qu'il abaissera le cas échéant, sur le combattant qui semble sérieusement en danger afin d'empêcher toute autre attaque. Son haume à crête est exposé dans le stand des dames. **F/G3** Chevalier disgracié forcé de s'asseoir sur sa selle, sur la palissade délimitant le lieu du tournoi. **F/G4** Les porte-bannières ne combattaient pas mais avaient besoin d'une bonne et solide armure lorsqu'ils suivaient leur maître au coeur de la mêlée. **F/G5** La tâche de ce valet est de lancer le cri de guerre de son maître et de l'extraire de la mêlée le cas échéant. Celui-ci porte une armure partielle et un bâton de nature purement défensive. **F/G6** Ces hommes attendaient derrière la double rangée de palissades pour protéger leur maître, tombé au sol, au moyen de gourdins. Dans les stands se trouvent les juges et les dames. **F/G7** Portant un baton blanc de service, le juge a part du stand du roi d'armes—qui peut pourvoir l'information des chevaliers. Quand le juge eut fait un signe le roi d'armes criait trois fois, 'Coupez cordes', et la mêlée commençerait.

**H1, H2** Le Bastard of St-Pol et le Bastard of Foix combattent au sol. Ils ont jeté des lances et ils se sont jeté leur bouclier avant de finir par le *bec de faucon*; celui de H2 étant terminé d'une pointe fine, H1 jeta sa visière. **H3** Un héraut du duc de Bourgogne s'avance pour faire cesser le combat; il tient à la main une corde servant à mesurer. **H4** Des hommes d'armes portant une armure complète séparaient les combattants, utilisant parfois des hallebardes.

**I1** Le haume et l'armure massifs portés pour le *Gestech* ne couvraient pas les jambes, qui étaient protégées par les grands rebords de la selle. Cette selle possède un troussequin bas qui permet de la démonter plus facilement. **I2** Cet écuyer, dans l'habit extravagant de l'époque, aide son maître à porter sa lance. **I3** Le maréchal, l'homme d'armes et le héraut étaient les responsables du terrain où se déroulaient les joutes.

**J1** Le roi Henri VIII et son opposant (**J2**) portent des armures flamandes. Une haute barrière de bois sépare désormais les combattants. Sur l'illustration d'époque qui a servi de base à cette planche, Henri brise sa lance sur le heaume de son adversaire, mais la 'feuille de résultats', qui nous est parvenue, montre qu'en fait les choses ne se sont pas passées ainsi! Les personnes de la suite du roi (**J3**) portaient probablement des habits jaunes et violets.

**K1** L'empereur prend part au *Geschifttartscherennen*, la joute 'du bouclier qui disparaît'. Sa main droite est protégée par la plaque de la lance, que le combattant laissait tomber dès qu'il avait fait mouche. A noter l'absence de protection sur les jambes. **K2** Lorsqu'il était frappé correctement, le bouclier était projeté en l'air par un mécanisme à ressort qui libérait également des segments de sa surface.

## Farbtafeln

**A1** Teilweise rekonstruiert nach einer Figur aus dem 13. Jahrhundert. Wappenrock-Farben entsprechen nicht dem Wappen des Marschalls von England. **A2** Neuer zylindrischer Helm, sehr moderner Schild—beide mit dem Löwen von Flandern. **A3** Fussoldaten durften in dieser Zeit aktiv teilnehmen. Er trägt den konventionellen 'Kübelhelm' und gepolstertes *Aketon*.

**B1** Seidener Wappenrock über vergoldetem Lederpanzer, und ein vergoldetes und versilbertes Schwert aus Fischbein und Pergament; siehe Wappen auf *Aillettes*. **B2** Er trägt das Gerät seines Herrn und ist unbewaffnet, abgesehen von gesteppten Schenkel—und festen Schienbeinschützern. Helme für Bannerträger dürften gerade damals aufgekommen sein. **B3** Beruhend auf seiner bekannten Figur; sein Panzer ähnelt dem der anderen, aber sein Helm ist nur versilbert; in den erhaltenen Beschreibungen werden keine Lanzen erwähnt, dafür aber Schwerter an Ketten.

**C1** Der Grossteil des Körpers wird durch einen Plattenpanzer geschützt; ein enger *Jupon* über einem Ledermantel, mit daran befestigten Eisenplatten über einer Halsberge und *Aketon*. Es gibt wenig Unterschiede zum Kampfpanzer, aber siehe schweren Manifer-Panzerhandschuh links. Der weisse Hirsch kennzeichnet einen der Herausforderer unter Richard II. **C2** Sie führt ihren Ritter an einer Kette in einer Prozession solcher Paare; auch sie trägt Farben und Abzeichen des Königs. **C3** Er reitet das Pferd seines Herrn am Ende einer Prozession solcher *Destriers*. Siehe Verstärkungsplatte an der linken Seite von Sir Johns geschmücktem Helm. Dieser Squire trägt die neueste Mode—ein *Houppelande* mit hohem Kragen und ausgezacktem Rand.

**D1** Wie viele andere Bilder haben wir dieses aus dem Buch von König René. Hermelin auf dem Heroldsrock identifiziert die Bretagne; das Pergament an seiner linken Schulter zeigt die Wappen der beiden Hauptgegner und der Kampfrichter. **D2** Er ist gekennzeichnet dadurch, wie er seinen Heroldsrock trägt. Er kündet das bevorstehende Turnier an, während zwei kleine Schilde mit den Wappen der Kampfrichter den Gegnern überreicht werden. **D3** Er zeigt das Wappen seines Herrn, Lord von Gruthuyse; siehe starken panzerschutz und *Baselard*-Dolch.

**E1** Das Wappen des Lords von Charny ist auf dem Wandteppich zu sehen; die, die seine Herausforderung zum Kampf annehmen, geben ihre Namen über Herolde bekannt—hier **E2** ist der Herold von Diego de Valiere und er berührt den schwarzen Schild um zu zeigen, dass sein Herr zu Pferde kämpfen wird; der violette Schild ist ein Symbol für Kampf zu Fuss. Der Sporn wird als Anzeichen des Kampfeswunsches überreicht. **E3** De Valiere, ein Ritter von Kastilien, sieht von einer Sänfte aus in voller Bewaffnung zu. Solche theatralische Auftritte waren üblich.

**F/G** Das Mêlée oder Handgemenge, Mitte des 15 Jahrhunderts, nach detaillierten Bildern aus dem Buch von René von Anjou. In diesem Kampf zwischen etwa 20 Mann von jeder Seite werden keine Lanzen verwendet. **F/G1** Der Herzog von Bourbon, ausgerüstet für den Keulenkampf, bewaffnet mit *Baston* und einem stumpfen Schwert an Schnüren; er trägt einen Lederpanzer und ein Helmgitter, das für diese Kampfart typisch ist. **F/G2** Der 'Ehrenritter', ausgewählt von den schönsten Damen, trägt ein gesticktes Tuch an seiner Lanzenspitze; er wird dieses über jedem Turnierkämpfer senken, der in ernsthafter Gefahr zu sein scheint, um weitere Angriffe auf diesen zu verhindern. Sein eigener geschmückter Helm befindet sich auf der Damentribüne. **F/G3** Entehrter Ritter, gezwungen, rittlings auf seinem Sattel auf der Pallisade des Turnierfeldes zu sitzen. **F/G4** Bannerträger kämpften nicht und brauchten daher guten panzerschutz, weil sie ihren herren tief in das Gefecht hinein folgen. **F/G5** Er muss den Kriegsruf seines Herrn rufen, und ihn auch wenn nötig aus der Gefahr schleppen! Er ist teilweise gepanzert und trägt einen rein defensiven Stab. **F/G6** Diese Männer warteten zwischen den Doppelpallisaden, um ihre gefallenen Herren mit Stäben zu schützen. Auf den Tribünen sitzen die Kampfrichter und die Damen. **F/G7** Der Kampfrichter träft einen weissen Stab—sein Würdenzeichen. Er teilt die Loge mit dem Oberhaupt der Herolde, der ihn mit Informationen über die streitenden Parteien versorft. Auf ein Zeichen des Kampfrichters, ruft das Oberhaupt der Herolde drei mal 'Coupez cordes', dann beginnt das Melee.

**H1, H2** Der Bastard von St. Pol und der Bastard von Foix im Kampf zu Fuss. Sie haben ihre Speere geschleudert, und auch ihre Schilde, ehe sie mit *Bec de Faucon* zu kämpfen begannen—der von H2 hat einen dünnen Dorn, weshalb H1 sein nutzloses Visier zwecks besserer Sicht fortwarf. **H3** Burgundischer Herold mit Messseil will die Kämpfer trennen. **H4** Voll gepanzerte Männer reissen die Kämpfer auseinander, manchmal mit Hilfe von Hellebarden.

**I1** Der für dea 'Gestech' getragene massive Helm und Panzer—letzterer reichte nicht bis zu den Beinen, die durch Sattelverlängerungen geschützt waren. Der Sattel hat einen niedrigen Knauf für leichteres Abwerfen. **I2** Ein Squire in der extravaganten Kleidung jener Periode hilft seinem Herrn mit der Lanze. **I3** Der Marschall, zusammen mit einem Konstabel und einem Herold hatte die Aufsicht über den Turniergrund.

**J1** Heinrich VIII. und sein Gegner (**J2**) tragen beide flämische Panzer. Ein hoher Holzzaun trennt jetzt die gegnerischen Reiter. Die zeitgenössische Illustration, von der wir unser Bild haben zeigt, wie Heinrichs Lanze am Helm seines Gegeners zersplittert—aber das erhalten gebliebene Turnierblatt sagt, dass dies in Wirklichkeit gar nicht geschah! Die teilnehmenden Knappen (**J3**) trugen wahrscheinlich Gelb und Violett.

**K1** Der Kaiser reitet in das 'Geschifttartscherennen', das 'Turnier des verschwindenden Schildes'. Die rechte Hand ist durch die Lanzenplatte geschützt; die Lanzenplatte geschützt; die Lanze wird sofort nach Erzielung eines Treffers fallen gelassen. Sie Fehlen jeglichen Beinpanzers. **K2** Bei korrektem Treffer wurde der Schild durch einen Federmechanismus in die Höhe gedrückt, und Teile seiner Vorderseite sprangen ab.

**L1** L'armure dorée *Greenwich* de ce personnage porte son emblème 'du bâton déchiqueté' et elle est assortie d'un certain nombre d'articles destinés au tournoi, le *granguard*, le *pasguard* et le *manifer*. Dès la première moitié du quinzième siècle, les chevaliers devaient se serrer la main après le combat. **L2** Armure de tournoi provenant du nord de l'Italie; celle-ci est simple et fonctionelle. **L3** Le combat au sol avait lieu désormais de part et d'autre d'une barrière, de sorte que les jambes n'avaient plus besoin de protection.

**L1** Seine vergoldete Greenwich-Rüstung trägt sein Wappen—den 'schartigen Stab'—und ist mit Zusatzteilen für das Turnier ausgerüstet: *Grandguard*, *Pasguard* und *Manifer*. Schon in der ersten Hälfte des 15. Jahrhunderts wurde erwartet, dass sich die Ritter nach dem Kampf die Hand reichten. **L2** Eine Turnierrüstung aus Norditalien, einfach und funktionell im Aussehen. **L3** Der Kampf zu Fuss findet jetzt über eine Barriere hinweg statt, weshalb kein Beinpanzer erforderlich war.